BEING THE STARFISH™

For Network Marketing

6 PRINCIPLES FOR SHATTERING
THE NETWORK MARKETING STEREOTYPE

AND ~~SELLING~~ *SERVING* YOUR WAY
TO SUCCESS!

Neal Anderson

Being the STARfish™: 6 Principles for Shattering the Network Marketing Stereotype and Serving Your Way to Success
By Neal Anderson

Copyright © 2017 by Neal Anderson

ISBN-13: 978-197-1974032372
ISBN-10: 197403237X

Unless otherwise indicated, all Scripture quotations are from The Holy Bible, English Standard Version, copyright © 2001 by Crossway Bibles, a division of Good News Publishers. Used by permission. All rights reserved.

Scripture designated ISV taken from the Holy Bible: International Standard Version®. Copyright © 1996–forever by The ISV Foundation. ALL RIGHTS RESERVED INTERNATIONALLY. Used by permission.

Printed in the United States of America

REGISTER YOUR
STARFISH BOOK

to receive updates on
trainings, events & retreats
and receive FREE Tools!

GO TO:

BeingTheStarfish.com/NetworkMarketing

CONTENTS

SHATTERING THE STEREOTYPE

Your success and significance in life will be in direct proportion to the number of times you put others and yourself in a position to hear yes or no.

—Neal Anderson

Perhaps you're familiar with the parable of the sower. It's among the most famous of the stories Jesus told, and it begins with this simple statement: "A farmer went out to sow his seed."

Out the man went, reaching into the seedbag slung by his side and broadcasting handfuls as he walked through his freshly tilled field. (You can't get more hands-on than agriculture was two thousand years ago.) Thousands of seeds, scattered every which way and finding various landing places—bare dirt by the roadside, rock-cluttered hardpan, thick weed patches . . . and good, rich earth.

You can guess the outcome. Not all of the seed survived to bear fruit. That wasn't the seed's fault; it contained everything necessary to reproduce. The problem—and the promise—had to do with where the seed landed. Good seed minus the right growing conditions got eaten by birds, or it withered, or it choked amid the competition. But the seed sown in good soil flourished the way it was meant to.

Understanding this parable, Jesus told his disciples, is the basis for understanding all of his other parables. Why? Because the kingdom of heaven operates on the seed principle, to wit: You've got to actually sow the seed. You've got to make sure it lands in the right soil. And you've got to give it time, because seed doesn't just germinate, mature, and produce a crop in a day. It takes time and patience to reap a harvest.

Isn't that how so many things in life work? It's definitely the way direct selling works. Good seed, good soil, and action: furnish those three and you'll do fine.

Yet so many of us look for excuses to avoid the hard work and disappointing experiences. Faced with a challenge, we look for every way a possibility can't work rather than every way it's going to work. And in direct selling—and more specifically, network marketing—we don't want to hear the word NO! We want an easier way.

Network marketing *is* hard work. Most people equate hard work with physical labor. I know about physical labor. As a young man, one summer I worked at a sewer plant, shoveling processed crap and cutting brush at a small reservoir for $3.35 an hour while mosquitoes ate me alive. I also once spent an entire week splitting cement blocks and then stacking the halves on pallets—over and over, nine hours a day for five days—in order to pay for a muffler for my car.

To me those jobs were hard work.

Network marketing isn't hard in that physical sense. But it is hard work emotionally. It's often lived in the 6 inches between the ears. Done the right way, network marketing can bring tremendous blessings to you and your customers. However, you've also got the capacity to crash and burn—and many people do.

What makes the difference? How can you attain the life you dream of—a life well within your reach that enriches both you and others—versus letting your dream remain only a dream?

The answer begins with the next door, the next phone call, the next invite. But you have to knock. You have to take action. You have to get out and actually plant some seed.

So many people attend all the trainings and read all the books yet fail to see their business grow. They use personal development as an escape from doing the hard work. It's easy to read a book or take a program because there is no rejection. But you don't get a crop by reading books about farming—you get a crop by stepping out under the hot sun and planting seed.

The compensation plan is *doing* the activity that leads to creating customers and business builders. What's great about network marketing is, doing the fundamentals *is* the personal development program! And the best part is, you get paid to take the training!

The results you get from network marketing have everything to do with how you think about it, the way you approach selling, and the action you take. Because you're dealing with people—people who love to buy but hate being pressured to buy. People who want to know you care about them, not just what you want from them, and who need to trust you before they'll buy from you. People who resist being sold pie-in-the-sky opportunities but respond enthusiastically to being cared for.

Isn't that how you are too? Do you hate the thought of being a "pushy salesperson?" Moreover, your personal ethics won't let you promise the moon for the sake of a buck. Of course you want to make a living. But what you also want, very much, is to help people improve their lives with your products or services—because you know firsthand the good they can do.

A MORE FRUITFUL APPROACH

The most important skill you can learn in business is the ability to sell yourself and your ideas. The second is the skill to build relationships. And it takes the first in order to accomplish the second. Unfortunately, most people are not trained how to do this in a manner that enables them to work *with* human nature, not against it. So they struggle with needless blocks, fears, and self-esteem issues.

How about you? Do you loathe being in a selling situation? What if there's a much better way—and if there is, how can you put it in gear?

How can you trade methods neither you nor your prospects trust for a frank, servant-oriented approach that yields results both you and your customers will love? How can you exchange the unproductive habits of a SELLfish™ for the winsome and fruitful ways of a STARfish™?

Obviously I hope to show you. The tools for success I'm about to share with you have been forged, proven, and refined over my own long and successful career and in the careers of top mentors and coaches in direct and corporate sales. They simply work if you do. They're what have brought me from my days of selling door to door, 80 plus hours a week on straight commission for the oldest direct selling company to pay my way through college and law school, to working with lawyers and law firms selling Internet marketing, high net worth clients selling upper-echelon real estate, to clinical-grade sleep systems, and more. I've made thousands of presentations in all kinds of settings, from living rooms to corporate offices, and to people of every stripe—teachers, lawyers, doctors, farmers, retail employees, college students, married couples, single moms . . . the list goes on.

You can experience similar success with your own product, service, or opportunity. Not overnight, not without hard work and perseverance, and certainly not by accident. But if you will patiently cultivate the STARfish mindset and skills I'm about to show you, you will do well—because you will do things differently. No high pressure. No SELLfish practices that cost you both opportunities and relationships. Just a sane and empowering pathway to network marketing success.

Since my business is health and wellness products, I will reference it freely in my examples. Don't let that throw you—the principles apply across the board. Simply adapt them to fit your own product, service, or opportunity. You'll learn how to sell with energy and assertiveness out of a genuine desire to help people. You'll improve your sales acumen, your confidence, your lifestyle, and the world around you. Yes, you will step out of your comfort zone—but you'll also step into a much larger life of impact, fulfillment, and increased ability to bless and influence others. And you'll have a whole lot of fun in the process!

HOW TO USE THIS BOOK

Think of a playbook. You don't glance at it just once and then tuck it away. You consult it again and again.

Take your pen to this book. Highlight the parts that speak to you. Write notes in the margins.

And when you've mastered the principles so that they're part of your lifestyle, crack it open from time to time just to brush up. Use it to train your own team. It's meant to be that kind of resource: one that helps you develop not only yourself but also your team members by fostering the mindset, the skill set, and the personal development to excel not only in network marketing but in life. You have to learn how to lead yourself first before you can effectively lead others.

What follows is a logical, commonsense step by step process to cultivating the vital fundamentals that produce simplicity, duplication, and results.

Be warned: it's not all fun. It starts with forming the habit of doing the things you don't want to do. You do them anyway, regardless of how you feel. Remember the seed principle? You don't have to enjoy planting seed—you just have to plant it. That's what it takes to shatter the network marketing stereotype and get a bountiful crop.

CHAPTER 2

From Buckets to Pipelines: Building a Better Way

Your rank is never as important as who you become in the process.

—Neal Anderson

Big disclaimer: I am not on the New York Times Bestseller list. I do not have a fancy publisher. I don't even have to wear a suit at work! I'm simply one of you.

I've been through tens of thousands of noes to get where I am today. I know what it's like to have a door slammed in my face, to be rejected, to feel alone. I've stared at a prospect list not wanting to make the call. But each time, I picked myself up and focused on finding a way instead of an excuse. Action cures fear and creates confidence. My introduction to the world of sales (besides trying to sell my way with my parents beginning at age two) was as a ten-year-old living in upstate New York. The local YMCA had a free throw shooting contest, with a free membership going to the winner. Kids would knock on doors for a month to get folks to pledge a certain amount for every free throw a kid could make in a 15-minute period.

I knocked on every door I could find, often past dark. Some enthusiastic neighbors pledged up to 25 cents per successful shot. I filled up page after page with generous pledges. Then came the time to shoot the free throws.

Some would say I was a good little basketball player. I practiced nonstop in every driveway on the street. As the neighborhood's youngest player, I had to either suck it up or get beat.

Free throws were easy for me—so easy that I ended up making 149 in fifteen minutes and beat all of the high school kids and YMCA counselors.

Then came the time to collect the pledges. For fear of bankrupting our neighbors, my dad wrote a letter explaining my success and inviting people to give whatever they felt led to give instead of their committed pledge.

That was my first experience with setting a goal, sharing an idea, and then getting exactly what I pictured. I knew I was going to win.

After a 19-year retirement, I ran up to my first house again. This time I was in eastern Tennessee selling reference books and software door-to-door to pay my way through college and law school. For six hot summers, I knocked on doors and shared my ideas with people from all walks of life, socioeconomic backgrounds, and dialects. I was able to earn enough to pay my own way through school and have enough to do some pretty cool traveling. It was here that I learned how to be a STARfish™ instead of a SELLfish™.

After law school I was an account executive, selling law books, web-based libraries, and Internet marketing to law firms and government agencies for an international legal technology company.

Since that time I've had the good fortune to sell everything from high-end real estate, to clinical-grade sleep systems, to consulting services to health and wellness products! I've made over 50,000 sales calls and performed over 5,500 presentations in living rooms across the country. Add to that another 5,000 presentations in law offices and boardrooms during my 11-year corporate career.

And after all my years of experience in many different industries, I have yet to see anything as awesome as network marketing! What a blessing we all have to be in this profession!

In my previous occupations, although I was getting invaluable experience, making great money, and often getting those lucrative benefits, I was building someone else's company, someone else's dream. And day by day I was sacrificing mine. Can you relate?

I became sick of starting at zero every day, month, and year until finally it dawned on me—a transforming insight: *I was hauling buckets instead of building a pipeline.*

ARE YOU BUILDING A PIPELINE OR HAULING BUCKETS?

In his book *Rich Dad's Cashflow Quadrant,*[1] Robert Kiyosaki wrote about a man who carried buckets of water from a creek to a small town every day. He made this trip multiple times per day and could only increase his income if he hauled more buckets. The man had plenty of job security because the town needed a daily supply of water.

Then one day another man also started carrying buckets. Facing competition, the first man knew there was only one way to increase

---

1   Robert Kiyosaki and Sharon T. Lechter, *Rich Dad's Cashflow Quadrant: Rich Dad's Guide to Financial Freedom* (New York: Warner Books, 2000).

the amount of water he could provide: build a pipeline from the creek to the town. So he figured out how much money he needed to live on as well as pay for supplies to build the pipeline, and he used his spare time to build the pipeline.

Day after day, the first man hauled the requisite number of buckets to cover his expenses, and then he worked on the pipeline. The second man meanwhile continued to haul bucket after bucket into the little town, ultimately hauling more water than the first man.

After two years, the first man finally completed his pipeline. His first customer turned on the faucet and out came clean, cold water. Excited townspeople lined up, eager to purchase. All they had to do was turn on the faucet. Soon there were no lines, because people could get the first man's water whenever they desired.

The man realized he had built not only a physical pipeline to carry more water but also a financial pipeline which would enable him to leverage his time, treasure, and passions.

Are you building a pipeline or hauling buckets? I love this story because it demonstrates how powerful owning a business can be for a family as well as that family's community. It also brings to light how many in our society are trading time for money and a title and are often unfulfilled in the process.

Day after day, schools and universities promote the bucket-hauling mindset at the expense of people's dreams. Countless men and women get good grades, go to college, get a job, and then think they will retire on a nice income. Unfortunately, the days when that approach worked are long gone. Yet our educational factories are still tooled for it. And parents dig deep down in their pockets (or take loans) each fall to fill the addiction to more education instead of a practical model which will produce an asset instead of simply a job.

Back when I was hauling buckets uphill every day for the legal research company, I annually sold almost a million dollars of subscriptions, and year after year I woke up on the first of January sitting on zero. I had to start all over again. Can you relate? Of all those millions in sales I had made, I never saw a shred of residual income. My livelihood depended on my constantly pumping out new subscriptions. I had no leverage.

If I stopped working the next day, my pay would stop. That's when it hit me and something needed to change.

One day I added up all the reccurring revenue I had ever produced for my companies. I looked at how many customers had purchased from me. And I wondered: What if I had my own business, and my customers could be paying *me*, not someone else!

I wanted to leverage my time, my talents, and my treasures. I wanted to serve people a few times very well and get paid as they enjoyed the benefits of purchasing the products over and over. And that is what started my quest to build my pipeline instead of hauling buckets. The question now was, how?

THE CASHFLOW QUADRANT

In *Rich Dad's Cashflow Quadrant*, Robert Kiyosaki writes about how people make money in the world of business. He used the CASHFLOW Quadrant to explain a simple concept. Picture a square subdivided into four equal squares, or quadrants. At the top left is the letter E for *employee*. Under the E box is the letter S for *self-employed*. In the upper right corner is the letter B for *big business*. Finally, in the lower right corner is the letter I for *investor*.

The employee seeks security and prepares for it by getting good grades, going to a good college, and then getting a good job with the hope of retiring some day. Unfortunately, the day the employee stops working, the pay stops too. This is the model that most people learn and then live within.

Self-employed includes individuals like doctors, plumbers, contractors, lawyers. They own their business, but many say the business really owns them. If they don't adjust a back or fill a tooth or turn a wrench, no income is generated. Both the employee and the self-employed have something in common: their income stops the minute they stop working.

The big business owner has employees and often self-employed contractors building their business for them. This allows them to have more freedom as well as creating an asset that can pay them many years down the road.

The investor uses their money and other people's money to make more money.

As Robert explains, "Each of us resides in at least one of the four quadrants of the *CASHFLOW Quadrant*. Where we are is determined by where our cash comes from. Many of us rely on paychecks and are therefore employees, while others are self -employed. Employees and self-employed individuals reside on the left side of the *CASHFLOW Quadrant*. The right side of the CASHFLOW Quadrant is for individuals who receive their cash from businesses they own or investments they own."[2] Which side of the quadrant are you in?

---

2 Ibid, 2.

After reading this I realized that I was on the left side of the CASHFLOW Quadrant and badly wanted to figure out a way to get on the right side! I knew there was something inside of me that was off, but I didn't know how to explain it until I learned this simple diagram.

I was seeking a lifestyle somewhere between the security of an employee and the so-called freedom of a self-employed individual. I didn't want to have to check into a job every day, but I also didn't want the risk and headache of being self-employed. Being in direct sales allowed me to earn a great income and ability to set my own schedule, but I was building someone else's business, and I wanted to build my own.

So I went down the road of looking for a way to move over to the right side of the quadrant. I looked at everything from car washes to storage units to real estate to buying an existing business. And each time it seemed like I would only tie up a lot of money and leave myself with very little freedom.

Thankfully, my wife discovered network marketing through the recommendation of a friend, and the bucket hauling has been replaced by a pipeline of financial, spiritual, and time freedom.

A BETTER WAY

According to Gallup, approximately 70 percent of workers feel disengaged from their work, and a high percentage want to be doing something else. This has to change. Too many people are working too many hours for too many companies that provide little opportunity to create a great lifestyle—one that empowers people to fulfill their calling *and* spend more time with their families. The current work environment often takes people away from both their families and their dreams.

I am grateful that my wife took that first big step and created a network marketing business that enables us to serve people in a manner I believe God designed us for. Yet misconceptions abound about network marketing, aka multilevel marketing (MLM). And rightly so.

At a large company leadership retreat I attended, full of Silver rank and above, the speaker asked the audience, "How many of you said you would never do network marketing?" By my estimate, 99 percent of the room raised their hands. How about you? What was *your* opinion of network marketing before you discovered your company?

People's perceptions are often shaped by all of the opportunity peddlers who promote fancy cars and dream lifestyles rather than allowing the products and the retention rate to stand on their own merits. Too often, when people realize that the opportunity was unequally yoked with the product, the proverbial house of cards comes crashing down—along with years of trust and friendships.

In network marketing, we have the opportunity to share a blessing with people. And we can do it the right way. We get to *share* instead of sell. To *sow* instead of constantly feeling like we have to pressure the next person we see into joining a pie-in-the-sky opportunity. Network marketing is not perfect nor is it for everyone. But one thing is for sure: being a STARfish is about *giving* first without regard to what we may receive in the end. It is about stepping into the shoes of the customer and seeking to understand her needs instead of your own. The customer does not care about your rank. She doesn't care about the fancy car you may win. She cares about whether *you* care—about *her*.

There is an old saying: "Nothing happens until someone sells something." The problem with that expression is, selling is the focus. The motive is often to achieve a quota, win a trip or a car, or appease a pest of an upline leader. What happens to ethics and culture when production and rank are the priority?

Imagine if, instead, our primary goal was to understand others and help them get that which will improve their life's significance.

Servant selling is about being more concerned for others than you are for yourself, your company, or your bank account. When we break off a piping hot piece of our chocolate chip cookie and hand it to a friend, we do it not to win a contest, gain a promotion, or get a sale. We do it because we love this specific chocolate chip cookie experience, and we want to share it with someone else who we feel would love it as much as we do. Our intention is not to *sell* it but to *share it.* That is being a STARfish.

There are many ways to get from point A to point B hoping that someone will come to our way of thinking and believing. We believe our product can help someone. We believe it is the best option. But how do we persuade others without putting pressure on them or scaring them away?

This book will show you how and show you well. You will discover the difference between a *STARfish* and a *SELLfish* and identify a path to your calling. You will gain insight into the value of your time and learn how to accomplish everything you dream of with less stress. You will learn how people buy and how to "control the controllables." Finally, you will walk through each step of the sales cycle, from finding and connecting with new prospects to inspiring a roomful of future team members.

As Brian Moran and Michael Lennington write in *The 12 Week Year*, "Our experience has shown that most people have the capacity to double or triple their income just by consistently applying what they already know. Despite this, people continue to chase new ideas thinking that the next idea is the one that will magically make it all better."[3]

I'm not going assume that you already know the fundamentals and skills necessary to build your business and create a lifestyle that'll love to live. So I m going to teach you in this book. Once you understand the framework, you will be armed with what you need to get what you want. However, you will be tempted to reinvent the wheel—to look for that "next idea" or "the key." You will see people doing something that looks like it works and be tempted to stop doing what you *know* works; you will get distracted by the shiny object in the corner. But as author and speaker Randy Gage says, just because something works doesn't mean it duplicates. And duplication is the foundation to growing a team and having the freedom your team and you deserve.

You are going to have to work hard doing something for the next three to five years. You might as well work at building *your* dream and your business instead of someone else's.

My wish for you is that you will read this book with an open heart and simply believe you are worth it. Please use your God-given gifts, talents, and treasures to serve people the way God intended you to do. People are counting on you.

---

3 Brian Moran and Michael Lennington, *The 12 Week Year: Getting More Done in 12 Weeks Than Others Do in 12 Months* (Hoboken, NJ: John Wiley & Sons, 2013), 4.

THE MAN IN THE ARENA

It is not the critic who counts; not the man who points out how the strong man stumbles, or where the doer of deeds could have done them better. The credit belongs to the man who is actually in the arena, whose face is marred by dust and sweat and blood: who strives valiantly; who errs, who comes short again and again, because there is no effort without error and shortcoming; but who does actually strive to do the deeds; who knows great enthusiasms, the great devotions; who spends himself in a worthy cause; who at the worst, if he fails, at least fails while daring greatly, so that his place shall never be with those cold and timid souls who neither know victory nor defeat.

—Theodore Roosevelt

BEING THE STARFISH™

When your heart is on service you are never nervous.

—Creig Soeder

ellfy the SELLfish was giddy with excitement. His very first network marketing company! He couldn't wait to get started. Granted, he felt a little nervous, but he thought, "How hard can it be? I'm a good talker and I'm *great* with people."

Out Sellfy charged, beating the bushes for enrollees in his hot new opportunity. No need to use the company material—why bother. Sellfy had confidence. Charisma. A great product. He'd do things *his* way.

But an astonishing thing happened: people weren't interested. How could that be?

"Maybe I need to know everything about the products before people will listen to me," Sellfy thought. So he started memorizing the products, learning their chemistry. And day after day he hit the local coffee shops and home improvement stores, hoping to uncover a hot prospect. But no luck. People weren't buying. He even attended other people's network marketing meetings in hopes of trying to lure attendees to his company.

Next, he had an idea. He heard once that he could go where people hung out and act like he knew them. He would strike up a conversation and then slip in a short pitch about his company. He walked up to one person pretending to know them. "Hey, don't we go to church together?" No luck. He went up to another. "Hey, aren't you a doctor at Duke University Hospital?" They saw right through him.

So it went for two discouraging weeks—and then, suddenly, inspiration hit. Social media! Surely that was the key. Why hadn't he thought of it before! With renewed vigor, Sellfy blasted Facebook, Twitter, and Instagram with specials, deals, and ads hoping to lure someone, anyone, into hearing his pitch.

Still no good. No one wanted to talk to him. Actually, he noticed that his "friends" list was going down.

Sellfy's confidence and enthusiasm were dropping like thermometer mercury on an Adirondack winter night. Finally, discouraged and at his wit's end, he decided to talk with one of the company's top leaders.

Sherri the STARfish had a bounce in her step and a great attitude, and she always seemed *happy.* She also had a large team of customers and business partners. In her office, Sellfy poured out his frustration. "Sherri, I've been miserable," he confessed. "I'm trying my hardest, but no one wants what I have. I just don't get it. Is my town saturated? Is it a bad time of year? Is it because of my upline leader?"

"Sellfy, did you pay attention to your team's training?" Sherri asked gently.

"I didn't go. I figured it was all a bunch of hype, so I skipped it. Did you go, Sherri?"

"Of course I did."

"What did they cover?" Now Sellfy was genuinely curious.

"The presenters taught us how to succeed by using duplicable systems. They also said that many people would try to wing it, try to do it their own way, and those people would get frustrated. They told us to not reinvent the wheel but trust the systems. Things would go better that way, and if we did a few things right over and over, we would be successful."

Sherri talked about serving instead of selling. About how people love to buy but dislike being sold. About the difference between being a STARfish instead of a SELLfish.

"SELLfish focus on selling and on getting what they can get instead of giving what they can give," Sherri said. "They have a heart of scarcity instead of abundance. They complain about things that are out of their control, and they're usually the first ones to brag about a new rank or company car they just won. They also focus on their own needs instead of the customer's needs, and they usually wing it when faced with using a system."

Sellfy winced. *Bullseye.*

Sherri continued. "SELLfish create a high-pressure selling environment. They fail to take corrective criticism when there is room for improvement. They don't understand how people buy, and they usually overpromise and underdeliver."

Sherri smiled. "There's another, much more fruitful way."

"And that is?"

"Being a STARfish. Someone who focuses on sowing, on giving from a heart of abundance.

"STARfish control the controllables and focus on activity instead of results. They are extremely coachable. They focus on other people's needs, and they always use duplicable selling systems and teach them to their team.

"STARfish create a sharing environment by letting people feel comfortable saying no if the product or service is not a fit. They have learned how people like to be taken through the buying process in a way that puts everyone at ease. And they always *under*promise and *over*deliver."

Sherri leaned back in her chair and looked at Sellfy, and for a moment, there was silence.

Sellfy stared at the floor. "I've been doing everything all wrong," he finally said. "I've been so focused on myself that I haven't taken the time to figure out what the customer wants. I haven't been coachable. And I've been doing way too much talking and not asking enough good questions in order to fully understand what people want."

"So how will you change that?"

"Honestly? I'm not sure how to go about it, Sherri."

"How about if I were to give you some personal coaching? I can walk you through a duplicable process that will get you back on track. There's no reason why you can't fulfill your dream of helping people and being financially free. You just need a little guidance."

"Seriously? You'd do that for me?"

"Yes, Sellfy. I believe in you, and I know you can be extremely successful if you'll just do several basic things.

"But for starters, I want to address a few matters so we can be on the same page and you can have the very best experience. In order for you to have the best experience and for you to get the most benefit out of our working together I want to let you know what you can count on from me. First, I will always believe in you. When you tell me that you want to reach a certain rank, or hold five presentations a month, or whatever goal you set, I'm going to believe you can do it.

"Second, I will always be positive. I know how tough it can be to talk to people and not always get the result you hope for. So you need to know that I will be your biggest cheerleader and our time together will be uplifiiting and positive.

"Third, Sellfy, I'll always level with you. I will tell you what you need to hear, not what you want to hear. This is for your benefit, not mine. Sometimes leaders won't tell you what you need to hear, and that holds you back.

"Fourth, I will never ask you to do anything I'm not doing or haven't done a million times. Too many people will try to give you advice when they have never done what you are doing. Especially family members and friends! But you can trust that if I ask you to do something, it's not just theory. It works! How does that sound?

"There are only six fundamentals it takes to prosper in our business and six principles to master. If you do them, then you will succeed and help a lot of people in the process. This isn't magic. It's a formula. It's a system, and when you learn the system, you will live your dream.

"You can either work with human nature or against it. This system will help you work with it.

"So if you want to be not only successful but also significant, here is what I need to count on from you. First, I need you to be extremely coachable. When I ask you to read a book or attend a meeting or learn a technique, you have to trust that I won't recommend anything unless it will help you a ton. Maybe one of my suggestions will strike you as silly or unnecessary. Please trust me that it works and do it anyway. Remember, you don't need to *feel* like doing something in order to do it!

"Second, I need to count on you to always be positive. Positive around other teammates, positive with customers, positive at home, and positive in presentations. Your attitude will determine your altitude.

"Third, I need to count on your working hard. When your schedule says it's time to work on your business, I need to trust that you'll do so. You'll make the calls, invite the people, and do the presentations. I promise, the customers will take care of themselves if you do your best.

ı, I need you to study hard. Study your scripts, study your
nd make sure you are a student of this business.

I need to count on you to always level with me. Let me
know what is really going on. That is the only way I can help you.
You can always talk to me. One thing we do on our team is this: If
you're having a bad moment—we don't have bad days—you simply
'puke up.' *Up*, okay? Never across or down. If you have an issue with
something, call me and we will work it out. Don't call someone below
you on the team or someone on another team. Just call me. I promise
we can work it out and find a solution.

"But before you call me, whether it's about an issue or with a
question, I want you to ask yourself three things: What is the situation?
What are my options? And what do I think I should do? I'll bet that
most of the time, you will find the solution yourself. If you need
another opinion once you've gone through the questions, then call me
and tell me which option you feel would be the best.

"Finally, be someone who finds a way instead of an excuse. You
will be tempted to make excuses—because anything worth anything
involves hard work, frustration, and persistence. You may want to
give up. But you are going to be the type of person who finds a way.

"Can I count on you to do these six things, Sellfy?"

"You bet!"

"Excellent! Because if you do, then you will get where you want
to go.

"Now, one last question: Can I hold you accountable to do all of
these things the best you can?"

With a grin, Sellfy shook Sherri's hand and looked her in the eye.
"I'm all in," he said.

CHAPTER 4

PRINCIPLE 1:
DEFINE YOUR VISION

*Your vision is often developed as you do
the things you don't feel like doing.*

—Neal Anderson

What do you want? What would you do for no money? Why would you do it? In his excellent book *Start with Why*, Simon Sinek made the case that people don't care about what you do. They care why you do it.[4] Yet many of us in sales communicate in terms of *what*—what products we sell and how one feature or benefit is better than another—while failing to ever let people know *why* we are doing what we do. Yet if that question goes unanswered, our prospects are unlikely to connect emotionally with our *cause*. And it's that emotional connection that creates customers. So what is your cause? What does your company stand for? Do you know why you do what you do?

---

4 Simon Sinek, *Start with Why: How Great Leaders Inspire Everyone to Take Action* (New York: Penguin).

Most people in a company or organization know *what* they do, says Sinek. Fewer people know *how* they do it. (For example, a person in the shipping department may not understand the complete manufacturing process.) And very few in most organizations know *why* their company does what it does, which may explain the low level of employee engagement which Gallup perennially reports.

Sinek illustrates the what/how/why concept and its ramifications graphically with his "Golden Circle": three concentric circles which show how most companies communicate. The outer circle is what a company does; the next circle is how the company does it, and the inner circle is why.[5]

Most people and organizations communicate from the outer ring and work their way in. For example: "We sell health products" (What). We teach classes about their benefits" (How). Do you want to buy some?" (There's no Why). Not very inspiring.

But what if we reverse that order and communicate from the inside out, starting with Why, as Sinek suggests. Now we're speaking to the emotional part of people's brain, where buying decisions are made. When we do that, we inspire people and help them feel excited about our cause—because they're experiencing us as a STARfish, not a SELLfish.

Here is how the conversation might go when you start with Why:

"In everything we do at ——, we believe in thinking differently. We challenge the status quo. (That's the Why.) The way we do this is by making natural products that are safer, cheaper, and more effective than traditional healthcare options. (You've just explained the How). We just happen to make wellness products. Would you like to buy

---

5 Ibid, 37–39.

some, or maybe come to a class to learn more about how they can help you? (Last of all, there's the What)."

You see the dramatic difference between leading with Why instead of What? Why is inspiring; What, on the other hand, is less inspiring when it's out of order.

THE INTENTION CYCLE™

People want to know your intention for doing what you do. They want to know what you believe. Why are you calling to invite them to a class, party, or presentation? Is it only so you can make money off of them, or do you genuinely have their best interests in mind? For instance, do you care that they have the tools to provide their family with safe, effective, and affordable wellness options (or whatever your company's value proposition is)?

The Intention Cycle™ shown here illustrates the relationship between your Why, which is central, and the sequence of relationship building that your Why has the potential to generate, beginning with intention and culminating in enrollment.

The Intention Cycle is integral to the STARfish way of life. When people know your intention, they become interested in you and in what you have to say. Their guard goes down. They begin to like you, and from there, they come to trust you, which leads to respecting you, which leads to a relationship. The fruit of that relationship *may* be an enrollment. If so, wonderful! But if not, that's okay, because you're dealing with a person you truly care about, not just a potential source of income.

This process can take seven seconds, seven minutes, seven days, or never. The sooner people know why you are doing what you do, the sooner you can help them obtain something that could change their lives. You've got to cultivate credibility before you talk about your products and how great they are. Otherwise, as you describe those products, what your prospects are mostly hearing is your lack of concern for them as people. Internally, they're asking, "Do I trust this person?" "Is what they are saying even true?" "Why exactly are they inviting me to a presentation?" "What is their intention?"

Disregard for the Intention Cycle on the part of those in sales has left many people with a negative impression of our profession. They've tasted the SELLfish side of sales—but you can give them a better experience. Communicating your intention quickly will open up skeptical individuals to a whole new world of possibilities.

YOUR WHY—AWAKEN. DEEPEN. FULFILL.

In his book *It's Your Call*, Gary Barkalow writes, "What you were created to do is revealed in the form of your desires."[6] Those desires, says Barkalow—the Whys that lie behind what you do—unfold in a three-part pattern of awakening, deepening, and fulfillment.

God has a journey for every person, and that journey has many different paths, not just one. But every journey follows a similar trajectory: God *awakens* a desire in your heart, and you take a first step, and then another, and another.

There's a difference between desire—your Why—and your *calling*. Your calling involves the way God has wired you. It is a constant that resides in your heart, something you can't turn off that is larger than any one occupation or job. Your Why, on the other hand, forms in the process of doing something with increasing expertise, and you find fulfillment in doing it well. *Why* is about your intention for doing something, and it is prone to change.

What desire—what Why—has God awakened in you? As you put it in motion, you gain an education and experience by *acting*, and you get better at what you do as a result. You're *deepening* your

---

6   Gary Barkalow, *It's Your Call: What Are You Doing Here?* (Colorado Springs: David C. Cook, 2010), 64.

knowledge and ability—and the more proficient you get, the more satisfaction you experience in what you do and the more passionate you feel about it.

Ultimately, God uses your perseverance and faithfulness to bring about the *fulfillment* of your original desire—and then he calls you higher by awakening you to something new, and you start all over.

Let's say, for example, that God stirs in you the desire to share your company's products. You deepen this desire by educating yourself, teaching others, and serving customers. In time, you arrive at the point where your products are paid for every month. You've gained knowledge and expertise, deepened your abilities as a presenter and educator, and perhaps now God awakens in you a new desire to build a team. Thus you acquire a new purpose, a new intention. Your Why begins to change.

UNLESS—and here's the big pitfall—unless you quit before you have fully deepened your original desire.

Which, unfortunately, is what most people do.

Why? Because the part of the process that involved actual work didn't *feel* good. It just didn't feel exactly right.

There is a school of thought in many circles that you have feel this great, glowing "Why" in order to do anything. If you don't, then you must be in the wrong spot.

Wrong! The feeling comes only after you put in the hard work! Remember the seed principle? You don't plant seed because you feel like a farmer; you feel like a farmer after you plant the seed, and you do the hard work of farming, and over time you see your effort pay off in a harvest. *Now* you feel like a farmer—because you did more than just sow and nurture the seed. You also sowed and nurtured your desire to raise a crop. Come rain or shine, as you daily did the work of farming, you were also deepening your vision. Now you're reaping the fruit. And next growing season, you'll be much more motivated to plant seed—even when you don't "feel" like it.

That's how it works. Unfortunately, countless people who have a desire won't put in the work necessary to deepen their desire to the point where they get good at it. They've bought the fantasy that pursuing a desire shouldn't feel so much like work. So rather than pay their dues, they look for another job, or the next shiny object to chase, only to go through the same thing again. For too many people, quitting has become a habit.

THE COMPANY WHY VERSUS YOUR WHY

If all the people at Apple stopped making computers and started making jet skis, the jet skis they turned out wouldn't look anything like what we're used to. That's because Apple's company Why is to challenge the status quo and think differently, whether the product is computers or jet skis or a better mousetrap. Apple attracts people who believe in what Apple believes. They need the ability to challenge the status quo and think differently. Without it, the workers would likely become disengaged in an average company. But allowed to think differently and challenge the status quo, they will likely be fulfilled—at least for a while.

In direct sales, *you* are the marketing and sales departments, and therefore, you are the company. Prospects want to know your *personal* Why. Do you know what it is? What inside you would find fulfillment regardless of whom you did it for, as long as you could do it?

Unlike the big-picture Why that motivates a company such as Apple, your personal Why is prone to evolve. Life is a constant revealing of new desires as you fulfill previous ones, and your Why modifies accordingly.

So although it's important to define the motive that drives what you do (and the exercises you'll be doing shortly will help you do just that), you should start with the following understanding. Underline it, circle it, and highlight it with a big orange marker: *You don't need to have your Why all figured out in order to start doing what you do.*

Action creates your Why, and your Why isn't static. It will evolve as you continue to act. So if you want to discover your Why, put yourself in motion.

And bear this in mind: your Why is developed as you do things you don't feel like doing. Do them anyway. Out of them will emerge the passion and fulfillment you're looking for, the oil that fuels your torch. There are no shortcuts, and there is always pain in any beginning. But pressing on despite a lack of clarity will produce the clarity and purpose you desire.

Unfortunately, many people put the cart before the horse. Their Why-focus causes them to act only when they feel like it. And when they don't feel the burning passion of a Why, they do nothing—or worse, they make excuses. That's the danger of focusing inordinately on your Why: doing so can paralyze you when you need to be in motion, and just as bad, it can make you self-focused.

Loving God and serving people is the taproot of an awesome life; loving what you do is simply the fruit. Remember, it's not about you. You will find your fulfillment as a result of deepening and fulfilling the desire God puts in your heart.

With that said, it's important to understand what motivates you to do what you do. You need to understand your Why, and we're about to get into that.

The right kind of Why isn't defined merely by the things you think you want—that's too small a motive. *A Why worth living for is always about something bigger than you.*

DEFINE YOUR VISION/DEFINE YOUR CALLING

Take time to think through the following questions. Space is provided to write down your answers, but don't feel limited. Use a separate piece of paper or even a notebook if you need more room. The best experience is to have someone interview you by asking the following questions and helping you dig deeper by asking *why* after your answers.

Why are you working with your company?

I believe in the product. I believe in God given resources to heal oneself. I believe in working w/ doterra b/c they stand for good things & try to better 3rd world countries / supply sources.

What is the difference you can make in other people's lives by sharing your company's products and mission?

I can show them a natural alternative to over the counter or prescription meds to empower themselves w/o side affects. Also the tools & resources to help others & themselves by learning about the power of EO. Also ensuring you work w/ your Dr [illegible] their medical needs

How are people better off by having attended one of your classes, presentations, or parties?

Again - they learn the basic foundation about the what, how & why of EO. and get enough info to be intrigued to start their journey. They also can interact / build relationships w/ other like minded people.

What are some of the benefits of having your products in the home?

They are always accessible whenever you need them, for you, your loved ones, or to share w/ non users/believers.

How can your company improve the quality of your life?

- less time being sick/uncomfortable.
- Healing your issue at the cellular level vs masking it.
- less time at dr's offices, less expense
Oils are affordable.

What do you love to do?

I love to help people + share my oils + the benefits of them.

What are you passionate about?

What are your talents and gifts?

- Getting along w/ people
- Being able to relate to people
- Compassion
- believeability

YOUR DREAMS *in your Heart*

What are 25 things you would do if you had $5,000 more a month?

1. _Freeing - ~~all~~ bills paid off._
2. _date night regularly_
3. _Take more weekend trips_
4. _John new vehicle_
5. _re-do flooring_
6. _could move_
7. _have time w/ family_
8. _live balanced_
9. _____
10. _____
11. _____
12. _____
13. _____
14. _____
15. _____
16. _____
17. _____
18. _____
19. _____
20. _____
21. _____
22. _____
23. _____
24. _____
25. _____

What are three things you could do that would improve the quality of your life?

1. Get a job
2. Have sustainable income
3. Make regular calls / contact w/ people

What are ten things you want to accomplish in the next 12 months?

1. Grow business!
2. Get Builders
3. Sign people up on LRP
4. Get structure in order
5. $1500 mo payout | Silver
6. reactivate stalled customers
7. Get current leaders excited ab/dg!
8. 1000 instagram followers
9. get better at social media / mass communic
10. Sign business up (2) doterra
   - heavenly Massage or a spa, or hair salon
   - health club or chiropracter

What are three things you want to accomplish in the next 12 weeks?

1. Convert customers to LRP
2. reactivate stalled customers
3. Get new customers
4. Get Builders

Write out your ideal day if money or time were not an issue?

get up, breakfast, go to the beach
spend time w/ family

What will you have to sacrifice in the short term in order to live your dream in the long term?

1. _Time_
2. _Take a class: Aromatherapy_
3. _or in social media (webinars)_
4. _____
5. _____

Why will it be worth it?

Sustainable income
lifestyle ∆'s
happiness

What do you envision for yourself two years from today? What will you be doing? How will your circumstances have changed?

- Working FT.
- doTerra business, booming
  - Diamond level (Jan 2021)
- Paying off house → Building
- Saving $$
- Ramping up for retirement

TO-DOS

- ☐ Get 40 pictures that inspire you and speak to your heart.
- ☐ Narrow them down to 20.
- ☐ Place them on a poster board with enough space to write one word under every picture. Write a word that describes how you feel when you look at each picture.

CHAPTER 5

PRINCIPLE 2: VALUE YOUR TIME

You will never feel like doing something more than at the moment you know you should be doing it.

—Neal Anderson

W e all have the same amount of time each day, so why do some people get more done than others? STARfish know where their time goes, because time is money— or is it freedom?

Your need for assistance with time management is usually in direct proportion to the distance you are from your calling and the habits that you have formed. The further away you are, the harder it is to stay focused. Many time experts would have you believe you have a time-management problem when in fact your "problem" is only a symptom. The cause is that you are in conflict with your calling.

When you are living your calling, time is much easier to manage. You are drawn by your calling instead of fighting against a job that simply doesn't fit your values. Granted, we all need to push through tough times and do things we don't feel like doing. However, doing this every day for 40 years is a bit much for anyone.

The average American indulges in around 35 hours of TV and other media per week. Over a 10-year period, that is a total of—get this—18,200 hours!

Not impressed? Let's put it in more meaningful terms. Divided by 40, the number of hours in a typical workweek, those 18,200 hours translate into 9.4 *years* of working 40 hours per week at 48 weeks per year.

Did you get that? *Nine-point-four years* parked in front of the TV.

I am not condemning people who watch television. I have my own favorite show, and you will also find me plastered in front of the TV for many college basketball games and *all* of March Madness! But wouldn't you love to have that much time to do something productive? What would you do with some extra time?

One of the best ways to discover where your time goes is to complete the 168-Hour Exercise. This exercise will help you to

- Discover the value of your time.
- Identify the cost of doing specific daily activity.
- Plan for what you need and want to do.
- Very importantly, identify the time-eaters that are not getting you closer to your dream, so you can replace them with activities that will.

This isn't astrophysics. All you do is take each task and figure out how much time you spend on it, first every week, then every year, and then over a ten-year period. Then you assess whether that task is worth your time.

Once you've created your list and completed your assessment, you create a weekly schedule. You should approach it much like you did back when you were in high school. Remember? The bell rang and you went to math. The bell rang again and you went to science. You left science and had lunch, and so on until after school, when you either played sports or went home. At home, you did your homework and chores, ate dinner, and eventually went to bed. (Of course, your schedule might have looked a bit different if you were educated at home).

While you might have started your homework in math class, you didn't finish it there. There wasn't time. You went from class to class—and if you were like me, you had your stuff packed up five minutes before the bell rang!

With this example from school days in mind, let's get started organizing your hours in a way that can create a personal pathway toward goals attained and dreams fulfilled.

168-HOUR EXERCISE

Begin by making a list of all the things you have to do each day for an entire week—168 hours—from the time you get up until bedtime. Include things you would love to do but may not be doing currently, such as reading daily inspirational material, working out, playing the piano, or having a date night. (An online version of the following grid is available at www.beingthestarfish.com/networkmarketing)

Write down the number of hours you invest in each activity daily. (Since we're talking about 24-hour days, don't forget to include the time you spend sleeping at night). Then add the numbers for every activity together to get its weekly subtotal. Finally, add all those weekly subtotals together to get a grand total of all the hours you've accounted for in your week.

Now subtract that number from 168. How much time do you have left? That number will tell you whether you truly "don't have time"!

Activity	Hours Per Day	Hours Per Week	168

Total Time Remaining:_____

Let's say you wind up with 10 hours left over at the end of the week. Ten hours per week for 48 weeks per year multiplied by 10 years is 4,800 hours. Divide that figure by a 40-hour workweek and you get one hundred twenty 40-hour weeks. That's 2.5 years of 40 hour workweeks to do whatever you choose.

Now ask yourself, "How would my life be different if I spent those 10 hours per week doing what I love, or learning a new skill, or building my business?"

HOW MUCH IS YOUR TIME WORTH?

Ready for the final step? It's time to discover the cost of carelessly misusing your time. How much money are you losing? Ultimately, how much freedom? You're about to find out—so you can take steps to upgrade the value of your time to its true worth.

Determine your current or desired hourly income. If you have an annual salary, this table will help you figure out your hourly pay.

My desired or actual annual income: $200,000

Weekly rate (divide annual income by number of weeks you work per year): 4166   (48 wks)

Hourly rate (divide weekly rate by number of hours in your workweek): $208.30   (20 HRS pr wk)
104.15 = 40 HRS $75.74 /55 HRS

Now multiply your hourly rate by the number of hours you spend in each category on your list. For example, if you'd like to make $26.00 an hour — 53.00 @ 110K/ann — and you watch two hours of TV per night, you are actually spending $52.00 daily on TV, or $260.00 per five-day workweek—and that's not including the cable bill! If you pull over at the local coffee house and spend 30 minutes there, your $4.00 latte costs you $17.00.

Now ask yourself, "Is what I'm doing worth the money I'm spending to do it?"

NOTE: This exercise only applies to activities that are not relational or vital. Don't go figuring out how much it's costing you to have a date night with your spouse and then decide to bail! Relationships are beyond price, and spending time with a loved one is always worthwhile. STARfish understand perfectly the difference between activities that are worth their time versus those that are not.

On the next page, you'll find a list of controllable activities that a STARfish commits to doing every day to guarantee his or her success. STARfish know that a great day starts the night before by planning the next day and making a decision to have a great attitude, work hard, serve people and find a way!

EVENING

- Write out a call list of people to contact for tomorrow
- Write down activity stats
- Refill your supplies, paperwork, presentation bag
- Record expenses and mileage
- Review your scripts
- Read goals/vision
- Get seven to eight hours of sleep

MORNING

- Do 20 minutes of inspirational reading
- Review your goals and vision
- Have family breakfast
- Call two people and inspire them
- Exercise
- Pray

DAYTIME

- Be mentally present all day
- Make at least two new contacts
- Make at least two customer calls
- Make two calls to leaders
- Get product training
- Attend team call
- Coach leaders
- Be coached
- Teach at least one class or presentation per week
- Do 2–3 (or more) one-on-ones per week

To conclude, the following ten questions can help you simplify the above and give you a compass for your day.

10 DAILY QUESTIONS

1. What two things am I thankful for?
2. What two things am I committed to doing today?
3. Who am I going to share my products/service with today?
4. Who am I going to call and inspire today?
5. Who will I follow up with today?
6. Who will I share our loyalty rewards program with today?
7. Who will I share the opportunity with today?
8. What one thing do I want to learn today?
9. What will I give today?
10. What activity will I do today with my family, a family member, or a friend that will deepen our relationship?

(Adapted from Rod Richardson and Seth Risenmay's 6:3:1 success form

We stay in a comfort zone when we are more focused on ourselves than on a person we can serve

—Neal Anderson

CHAPTER 6

PRINCIPLE 3: CONTROL THE CONTROLLABLES

It's a lot faster to act your way into believing than believing your way into acting.

—Neal Anderson

What do you feel you can control? People often waste valuable energy worrying about things that either never happen or that are out of their direct control instead of finding a way to work with what is right in front of them.

SELLfish tend to focus on things outside of their control—for example, their sales location. SELLfish say things like, "If I lived in that person's state, I would be crushing it as well," or, "The only reason they do well is, all the leaders live in their town so they can get support."

Or SELLfish let the time of year be their excuse: "People aren't going to come to events or presentations in the summer. *Everyone* is on vacation!" "No one will come to my parties during the holidays. They are too busy." How many times have you used such an excuse to get out of doing something that could bring rejection—or even failure? That is often a tough wound to reopen.

STARfish know exactly what they need to do in order to make success 100 percent predictable. By repeating a proven system day after day, they remove the stress from their work. They know that a productive day begins the night before.

They also understand that there are only four things they can control:

1. Their attitude
2. Their schedule
3. Their work habits
4. How well they serve people

These four areas are what I call *controllables*, and they need no defining. Their meanings are obvious. If only they were as easy to live out as they are to explain! But tucked away inside us are factors that conspire to keep us from controlling the controllables. Things that can block your success if you let them.

But you don't have to let them.

Let's examine how these issues may be affecting you and how you can overcome them. We'll start with one of our most formidable opponents: the three-headed giant known as Fear.

THREE TYPES OF FEAR
FEAR OF REJECTION

Knowing your Why is important. But do you know your Why Not? People are often more paralyzed by their Why Not than they are by the lack of a clear Why.

Give me a person who has learned how to overcome their Why Not over a person with a strong Why any day. When you overcome the Why Nots in life, you'll discover your Why. But people allow excuses to keep them stuck.

The fear of rejection is a huge Why Not. If you don't experience it, then you are likely not doing network marketing correctly (or any job, for that matter). The point is to not let that fear immobilize you. People are often paralyzed by fear that never materializes. They cannot, for instance, get themselves to pick up the phone or approach a stranger because they are so afraid of what people will think about them. A wise sales manager told me long ago, "Don't worry about what people think about you. They are too busy thinking about themselves."

Fear of rejection reared its ugly head regularly during my door-to-door selling days. I faced it every time I knocked on the next door. But the fear was never justified: the people behind the doors just weren't as scary as I dressed them up to be in my mind. And eventually, I did not feel rejection because I learned how to change my definition of success. I also learned that action cures fear and creates confidence. And confidence creates champions.

One thing that helped was to separate what I was selling from who I am. I've learned not to take people's "No" personally. Some people will like what I have and others won't. It's not my job to talk them into something they don't want. My job is to make a list of people to invite and cross people off of it after I contact them. Some will understand the value of what I'm offering them while others will not. And that's okay.

In selling door-to-door, as long as I focused on seeing a lot of people and left everyone in a better mood than when I found them, it didn't matter to me which ones bought from me. The more people I talked with, the more became customers (funny how that works).

So I tried to collect as many noes as possible and leave every person feeling better for having talked with me. Sales were simply a matter of letting the law of averages work in my favor.

There are buyers on every corner in America. If you take your products or service and started knocking on doors in a nearby neighborhood, the law of averages says that three out of ten families will sign up. And I know firsthand that the law of averages works.

Thirty percent of people will always buy from you.

Thirty percent will never buy from you.

And forty percent are indifferent.

Many top leaders in network marketing say you don't need any skills or sales training to do well. This may appear true because of the 30 percent who will always buy. But why leave out the significant 40 percent who might be persuaded? If you begin to master the principles and techniques of sales communication, you can convert many of those "indifferents" to loyal customers and potential business builders. Mastering sales skills will make the difference between being an average performer versus a champion.

By all means, go for the 30 percent who are the low hanging fruit, and thank God for them. In the beginning, they will provide not only customers you can add to your team but also a way for you to practice the fundamental skills to succeed with the 40 percent.

As for the 30 percent who will never buy—the ones who give you a ton of objections and every reason why what you offer is a scam or won't work—why waste your time on them? When you focus on the 70 percent who will likely engage with what you have, and you develop the right skills, your fear of rejection will diminish.

So don't let the fear of rejection stop you. Instead, change your definition of success. When you learn to reframe every no as just one step closer to the next yes, you can be successful with every invite situation or presentation. So what if someone turns you down? You're still engaged in income-producing activity. That's success, is it not? Of course it is. You've narrowed down the odds in your favor, and you're closing in on helping your next customer. Congratulate yourself—you're right on track!

FEAR OF FAILURE

Does the network marketing business model actually work? Can you succeed at selling it? You would not be the first person to ask such questions. The answer to both of them is yes. And your success can be 100 percent predictable when you control the controllables.

There are many successful people in your company who have paved the way for you. Look around. They have the same products, the same training, the same compensation plan, and the same business model. What made the difference? They didn't let fear of failure keep them from their dreams. Instead, they have looked their fear in the eye and said, "Yes I can!" And upon their dreams they have built magnificent lifestyles. You can too. But it takes discipline. It takes work. It takes action when you don't feel like acting.

FEAR OF SUCCESS

Have you ever known someone who felt it was noble to be poor? Or who thought you have to sell your soul in order to be rich? This is simply faulty programming. Granted, money earned by unethical means is wrong. But wealth gained ethically enables you to do a lot more good in the world. So why do so many think it's more honorable to be poor than to have enough money to feed the poor?

Those who live in the paycheck world rarely get the freedom network marketers get. If you really want to change the world, go make a lot of money. Get that part out of the way so you can help a lot of people.

The following was a Facebook post by Betsy Holmes, a leader and Presidential Diamond in the company my wife and I work with. Betsy had been traveling to a rugby tournament in Bermuda with her husband and business partner, Paul, when they parked across the street from the second largest private yacht in the world. The yacht carried a $475 million price tag and was appointed with two helicopter pads, 24 guest cabins, several hot tubs, swimming pools, and a submarine capable of submerging to 50 meters. Approximately 70 crew members are needed to operate the yacht and serve the guests.

How much poverty could be alleviated with $475 million dollars, Betsy wondered. She wasn't being critical; that's something we're prone to do in the face of extreme indulgence, but for Betsy, the spectacle took her in a different direction. Here is what she said:

> I want to make it clear that I am not judging [the owners]. King Solomon was pretty extravagant, and I think that God is extravagant with us. After all, he created the most beautiful places on earth and beautiful human beings. And I think heaven will top any human-made ocean liner.
>
> Perhaps these billionaires see themselves as giving opportunity and jobs to many people because this boat was made. I don't know, and I don't care. For me, I think that amount of money causes one to dream and takes limitations off of things you never thought possible.

Well, if God owns everything anyway and has much more money than these billionaires, AND you trust him, then that means you are a son or daughter of the richest guy out there, who wants to bless you as his child AND bless you to be a blessing to others (also his children). And he doesn't always do that financially because he knows we have more needs than that—needs of the heart.

But, what does it look like for you if $ limitations are taken away? What would you do with $475 million? What is your REAL dream if all limitations were taken away. If it's not to buy a boat, then what is it? Whatever that is—it's your real dream that you maybe didn't think is possible. But that's your real dream! And I think it's possible! That amount of money, at least for most people, takes away thinking about themselves, because no one needs that amount of money just for themselves.

Sure, there are greedy people, and loving money causes all kinds of issues to one's detriment. For me, I know a whole lot of orphans who could use some protection from the world, a safe place to grow up, loving parents, etc. That is the direction I would go with this much $. But I don't view the money so highly or love it—because it takes PEOPLE to change lives, not just money. People who are willing to be the hands and feet of God. People who believe they already have what they need and just get started because they know their dad already has it.

The dream comes before the $ in most cases. Not all dreams even need money. So, like the guy at the end of the movie *Pretty Woman* said, "What's your dream?" Ha ha! This business guy's dream was to build an extravagant boat perhaps. What is yours? Helps me think about this, so I thought it might also help *you* to think on that beautiful dream of yours and stop using $ as the excuse.

So what is your negative programming that you need to change? Do you fear success? Failure? How about rejection? Do you have money blocks or simply *action* blocks?

Our subconscious is frequently in conflict with our conscious mind in ways that can hinder our growth. Unfortunately, the subconscious mind is just that: subconscious, below the surface. So if we want to change our beliefs, we need to change our programming.

PROGRAMMING

In his book *What to Say When You Talk to Yourself,* Dr. Shad Helmstetter discusses how the results we get flow out of what we tell ourselves.[7] Significance and success stems from our actions, which are determined by our feelings, which are based on our attitudes. And our attitudes come from our beliefs, which are simply a matter of programming.

If we buy into our fears, we will have false programming. If we develop the habit of being timid in the face of fear, we will forever remain stuck in life. If excuses appeal to us more than finding a way, we will perpetually have bad programming. And our bad programming will keep us from fulfilling our calling and helping a lot of people along the way.

Let's say you were told at a young age that all rich people are bad. You accept this as truth, and that belief shapes your attitude toward wealthy people. Since you feel negatively toward them, you act in ways that ensure you yourself don't become rich. You may form a

---

7 Shad Helmstetter, *What to Say When You Talk to Yourself: Powerful New Techniques to Program Your Potential for Success*, rev. ed. (New York: Gallery Books, 2017).

victim mentality. You begin to make excuses. You take the easy way out. You want more out of life, but you justify your failure to actively improve your situation, based on your belief that it's okay not to have what you want because being poor is somehow noble.

This mentality keeps us stuck. We tell ourselves, "No one wants to come to a meeting over the holidays." This affects our self-image, because we know deep down that people *will* come if we ask—and when people do not attend a meeting, we definitely won't get any results!

So now our confidence level is down. Instead of picking up the phone, we become paralyzed with fear. Fear of what people will say. Fear of getting rejected. Maybe even fear of being successful.

Something has to change. But what—and how?

SELF-TALK

We need to change our programming. And in order to accomplish that, we have to change how we talk to ourselves. We must become aware of our internal dialogue, assess it, and be careful about what agreements we make with it. For example:

"I'm not good at talking to people."

"People are too busy over the holidays to come to an event."

"Rich people are bad. Having money is the root of all evil!"

"No one has money in my town"

"I'm not a sales person"

"People don't like MLM"

These are not good things to tell yourself if you want to run a profitable business! If they've been programmed into your belief system, now is the time to deprogram yourself, because this kind of thinking will keep you stuck. The good news is, you *can* change your thinking by changing the way you talk to yourself and then simply getting into action mode.

Too often people blame their situation on their circumstances when in fact they have simply made a conscious decision not to act.

I was on my way up to New York to teach my first official class. Prior to this I had done a few one-on-ones and observed many classes, but that was it. I could have excused myself from having high expectations. I could have let my self-talk go something like this: "This is going to be scary! I wonder if anyone will show up—or even enroll. Do I even know enough about the products yet to teach a class? Maybe I should wait."

Instead I pictured a full living room. I saw people smiling and digesting the information. I told myself repeatedly that this was going to be the best class in the history of my company! I pictured every person filling out the enrollment form and breezing through each information box.

"They are going to love me, and they are going to love the products," I thought. "I'm going to serve them, find out each person's health goals, and then help them accomplish those goals." I told myself that I was coming home with ten enrollments.

This is how a STARfish talks to himself before he presents. And the fruit of my self-talk was a great evening for everyone, with eight enrollments.

So get out there and teach! If you can tell your story and understand a little bit about your company and its products, you will do fine.

You may feel like you are not ready. You may tell yourself that you will stink. But you *won't* stink, so turn that thought around and tell yourself just the opposite, because that's the truth. You're going to do great. Most people do not know what you know, and your attendees will think you're doing a fabulous job.

ATTITUDE

We have heard about the importance of having a good attitude since the day we first had a bad one. My dad, who was the greatest salesman I've ever met, used to tell me, "Neal, change your attitude." He himself always had the best of attitudes because he always focused on what he could control. He didn't make excuses—he just went to work. It's amazing what that simple, powerful combination of no excuses and hard work can accomplish! Action cures both fear and attitude issues.

Dad used to sell hospital beds for the Hill-Rom Company, which had about 90 percent share in their market. He worked his way up the ladder and ultimately retired as the senior vice-president of sales and service. Not too shabby for a guy who was born at the beginning of the Great Depression. My dad reached his level of success because he had a positive attitude; he always knew that something good would happen if he treated people right and simply went to work.

Showing up is more than half the battle. My dad drove through blizzards in upstate New York, Vermont, and New Hampshire to make calls on hospitals when most people would have made excuses and remained in the comfort of their home office. When he showed up in the middle of a snowstorm, do you think his chance of getting an order increased?

Dad simply refused to let a storm get in his way of helping people. He knew how easy an excuse is to make, but he chose to control how he perceived a situation. That's the attitude of a true STARfish—and attitude is everything. It's really simple. Have a good one.

CONFIDENCE VERSUS BELIEF

Confidence and *belief* are important terms, yet they're frequently misused.

Webster's dictionary defines *belief* as "a state or habit of mind in which trust or confidence is placed in some person or thing." Belief is important when we get started in any new endeavor. We need to have a basic understanding of what it is we are offering, how it is offered, whether our company will actually fulfill the order, and whether our company's culture is service-oriented or all about money and rank. We have to believe we made a good decision to partner with a reputable company.

Most of us would never attempt to create an income until we've made those determinations, and fortunately, the answers come quickly. Then, if you are in a company where the opportunity is at the forefront, you will present information to your customers that builds their belief in the company and its people.

What salespeople really need isn't belief but *confidence*: "a feeling or consciousness of one's powers or of reliance on one's circumstances."[8] Belief is just a first step toward cultivating confidence.

We believe a chair will hold us when we sit in it: after a few repeat experiences with chairs as kids, we rarely question whether a chair will support us. But selling a chair takes more than believing in it. Selling it requires a sense of mastery that empowers us to outwardly project expertise, care, and credibility as we show others how the chair will meet their need. That's confidence. Simply put, it's the conviction, born out of experience, that "I've got what it takes."

---

8   *Merriam-Webster's Collegiate Dictionary*, 11th ed., s.v. "confidence."

Confidence comes from taking action as we build the fundamental skills of our trade. In direct sales, those skills consist of finding people who aren't familiar with our product and taking them through a proven, efficient progression to help them make the best decision for themselves and their family. In doing so, we use a duplicable process— meaning that every salesperson can learn it, and needs to.

Confidence building follows the "learn/live/share/lead" model:

- You have a good personal experience with the products.
- You have a good experience with the company.
- You succeed at getting people to their first presentation, you get your first enrollment, you see that the process actually works, and your confidence begins to grow.
- You hear stories from customers who have a positive experience, and by and by, some of them present on their own and enroll more people. Now you've got a team!
- As your team members create a small income for themselves, your own income increases, and so does your confidence that the business part works.

It all hinges on executing the same simple activities over and over. It's like playing a musical instrument. You can read method book after method book and stare at reams of sheet music, but the only way you'll learn how to actually play the piano is to get your fingers moving. By practicing consistently, you develop muscle memory. After a while, your fingers simply know what to do. Your confidence goes up, and as you keep at it, you find that it's a whole lot easier to play in front of people.

"Nothing good happens until you want to give up," my dad often told me. "But you don't give up. You stick with it. And the feeling you're looking for happens on the other side of that. You have to keep going and get good enough at what scares you."

The first time I used one of my company's products, I realized, *Hey, this stuff works!* Talk about a belief builder! Nothing boosts your belief like knowing your product really is just that good.

As you advance in your business, your belief grows with you: belief in the product, the company, the leaders, the opportunity, and ultimately, in your personal ability to influence others to their benefit and yours. Your foundational belief evolves into a vision beyond what you can see when your products first arrive (or when you experience your company's service, if that is what they provide).

But belief only goes so far. Confidence is key, and it comes from taking *action*.

You don't need to overcome some block.

You don't need to "fully believe" in your product or company.

You don't need to attend one more self-development seminar or convention.

What you need is to act.

In network marketing, activity is your personal development program. Granted, you need skills and a framework within which to work—hence this book. It gives you all the tools you need. You don't need to read more books. Don't get me wrong—I'm all for reading and learning as much as you can. But don't get hung up on it. Because doing the work is what produces results, and results create the confidence and the excitement to do what you do. Take action and your confidence will grow.

Action trumps belief every time. The following six proactive steps will empower you to take action from the very start, even when you don't know all the ropes.

SIX QUICK STEPS TO BUILDING YOUR BELIEF AND CONFIDENCE

1. Focus on why you do what you do and on how it helps people. What if they don't change? What is the impact of their remaining the same?
2. Develop credibility by being a "product of your product." In other words, gain firsthand experience with the products you share by using them yourself and experiencing their benefits.
3. Put in a *ton* of activity. Activity breeds confidence *and* cures fear.
4. Know your intention toward your prospect and how to communicate it quickly.
5. Deliver on your promises.
6. Realize that everyone will be using your products eventually—and they might as well be on your team!

KNOWLEDGE PLUS ACTION BREEDS CONFIDENCE

Most of us have heard that "knowledge breeds confidence." The more we know about a subject, the more capable we feel in situations that require the knowledge we possess.

But it's acting on the knowledge that gives it teeth. The more times we put what we know to the test, the more often we do the things we know we should be doing and reap the results, the more confidence we gain.

And the more confidence we have, the easier it is for us to act—because we're getting better at what we do by actually doing it, over and over. We don't get better sitting on the sidelines reading game; we get better by being on the field *playing* the game.

Are you on the sidelines or out on the field?

Back in my door-to-door days, the first few times I ran up to a house and knocked on the door, I was scared! My sales acumen was formative and my confidence was low.

But as I took action time after time, I learned about human nature, mastered my approach, managed to get all the way through my presentation, and actually began to gain customers. And my confidence increased. The same thing will happen for you when people come to one of your presentations, buy some of your products, and end up sharing them with their friends.

CONFIDENCE IN A CLASS, PRESENTATION, OR PARTY

Confidence comes from action, but belief is the progression of stepping-stones that will spur you to action. The graph on the next page demonstrates how belief increases during the course of a presentation as an attendee gains knowledge.

Let's say you're that attendee. The first time you try your products, your belief in the product may be around 5 or 10 percent. (All percentages here are just guesstimates for the purpose of illustration.) Then you go to a presentation, and your belief begins to rise as you meet the host and presenter, see other people, and see the products.

The presentation starts. The host introduces the speaker, and your belief level gets another boost as you learn about his or her background, qualifications, and relationship with the host. As you relate to the speaker's story, and as you find yourself agreeing with their value proposition, your confidence in them and what they are doing rises to 40 percent. You begin to see yourself getting involved in whatever this "party" is about!

Once you start thinking about your goals and how they relate to the value proposition, you move still further up the confidence scale. By the time you've learned about the products or opportunity that can help you meet your goals, you feel about 75 percent convinced that you want to get involved.

Now the speaker summarizes what the presentation has covered, and that reinforces some of the reasons why the company and products/services would be a good fit for you. So you're ready when you hear the invitation, "Would it be okay if I shared with you how to set up your wholesale membership?" You bet! Boom! You sign up.

At this point you are about 85 percent sure you've made a good decision. When will you feel 100 percent sure?

One hundred percent certainty will arrive when you receive your products and have a few positive experiences with them. This is when a follow-up appointment to explain how to use the products can make or break your reaching 100 percent.

SHARING WITH OTHERS: THE CATALYST FOR TURNING BELIEF TO CONFIDENCE

Remember the day when you enrolled? Take a minute. What was it like signing the enrollment form? Leaving the host's house? Walking through your own front door and explaining to your spouse what you had just gotten yourself into?

If your spouse had inquired then about your desire to build a business, you might have replied that you had zero interest. But was it really your interest that was lacking—or your confidence that you could do it? With each new experience with your company, you likely became more interested and more confident in your abilities.

From the time you get your first products, your sharing journey follows a predictable path. As you experience the powerful effects of the products, you begin to tell your friends. Much as you'd do with a good movie or restaurant, you can't help but share with those who you feel could benefit from the same experience you've had. So share

CONFIDENCE
SHARING WITH OTHERS

100%

People Enroll   85%

Observe a
Presenation

People Show Up

Invite

Share

Experience

Enroll

Confidence

0%   Time

you do, and your confidence increases. You invite a few friends to a presentation, and they actually show up! Then as you watch your sponsor teach the presentation, your confidence rises and you think, "Hey, I can do that!"

At the end of the presentation, you feel excited. A few of your friends are actually enrolling! You're now about 85 percent confident that you've got what it takes to conduct a presentation yourself and even build a little team.

When will you be 100 percent confident? When you do a presentation and enroll your first person. This is why, if you are leading a team, it's critical to get your team members to each teach their own presentation and enroll their first person as soon as possible. Doing so will have a massive effect on their confidence as well as their ability to duplicate quickly.

Don't wait on the sidelines, hoping someone will knock on your door or private-message you with a request to enroll. Those situations may occur, but you can't count on them, and a passive approach will get you nowhere. You need to be active, and so do the team members you enroll. Guide them to the point where they can present and enroll people on their own. Because the ability to enroll others is what can change lives—including yours!

TWO TYPES OF PEOPLE

There are only two types of people in the world. One looks for a way; the other looks for an excuse. Guess which one is the STARfish and which one is the SELLfish.

It's human nature to cop out. Most people are experts not only at excuse creation but also at strategic execution. Finding an excuse is easy; finding a way is not.

We all face difficult situations at times. That is life. We may not always be completely responsible for what happens to us, but we are 100 percent responsible for how we respond. And how you respond is what will make all the difference. Will you find an excuse, or will you find a way?

Our family spent spring break on Hilton Head Island with some friends. Six months before, Hurricane Matthew had ripped through the island and wiped out many houses and a lot of trees. My wife asked our middle son, "Do you know why the palm trees survived?" He didn't. She explained, "The palm tree is designed to bend and withstand high winds. Each time the storms come, palm trees can bend almost to the point of being horizontal to the ground, but they won't break. After the storm passes, the palm tree will stand straight up again as if nothing happened. The more storms the tree encounters, the stronger it gets." At this point, our son's eyes were wide open. My wife continued, "The same thing is true of life. You will have to go through storms that sometimes seem impossible. But God made you able to withstand the storms, and like the palm tree, you will come out even stronger." ✱

It is easy to make excuses when things get hard in network marketing. You have to push through and realize that every time you find a way instead of an excuse, you get stronger.

During college and law school, I worked for the oldest direct-selling company in the United States, selling educational books and software door-to-door. Every summer when college was out, I used to attend the company's week-long, intensive sales and leadership school along with a host of other students from all over the United States. Once the school was over, we all went our separate ways to different parts of the country, found our own places to live, got up at 5:59 every morning, took an ice-cold shower, and then went door-to-door for 14 hours, six days a week, working on straight commission and paying all of our own expenses. There were no guarantees except that we would hear "No" a lot! One summer I worked hard enough to finish in the top 30 out of over 3,000 students.

That same year in the fall, I returned to Indiana University needing 45 credit hours to graduate. In order to begin law school the following year, as I had decided to do, I would have to take 23 credit hours one semester and 22 the next. Considering that full time is 12 to 15 credit hours, taking on so much coursework was a daunting proposition. And I was already spearheading a student sales group at IU for my company! So extra time was not something I felt I had.

But I wasn't going to let those concerns stop me. I knew I could find a way because I had developed the habit of doing so. I completed the necessary credits, graduated a semester early, and accomplished my goal of entering law school the following fall.

Throughout my six years selling books door-to-door (and throughout my selling career), I wanted to quit countless times. Fortunately, I had learned the STARfish's secret of controlling my four controllables: my attitude, my schedule, my work habits, and how well I served people.

Too often we fail to take responsibility not only for our actions but also our inaction. But the short-term comfort of making excuses catches up with us in the long run. Eventually we have to take responsibility for how we will react to life's challenges.

My personal decision to act and never quit has not only changed my life but also served as an example that helps thousands of others believe they too can push a little harder, knock on one more door, and take the yeses and noes in stride. The yeses pay the bills, but the noes build character, so don't let them discourage you. Wanting to quit is okay. Quitting is not.

We need to be people who find a way when it looks like we have no options. This country needs us. Our community needs us. Our family needs us to be the best we can be. There is always a way.

You can be a light. You can provide hope. You can provide inspiration and healing to so many people right in your community and around the world. People are hurting, and if we quit, if we fail to find a way, then others suffer.

Much of the joy that comes in this life results from having an attitude of gratitude and being that person who finds a way over, under, or around any obstacle. As Chris Brady from Life

Leadership says, "There is no safety in a significant life and no significance in a safe life."

WORK HABITS

STARfish concentrate on their work habits and activity, not their results. They control how hard and how smart they work, and they purposefully choose the activities on which they will focus.

Conversely, SELLfish focus on results, recognition, and what people think of them. Scrambling to achieve a higher rank, they sidestep honest effort and patience in favor of shortcuts. They sell on Amazon or blast social media and poach other people's prospects because they are too lazy to find their own.

STARfish know there are no shortcuts. Period. They know that the best way to get results is to break down the end result (an enrollment) into little activities that lead to an enrollment.

Those smaller activities are so important! That's why STARfish keep a log of how many contacts they've made, samples they've given out, invites they've given, presentations they've held, and many other significance-producing activities. (You'll find a list coming up shortly.)

When you know your numbers, you take the pressure off yourself, and then sharing is fun! STARfish find their self-esteem in work habits, not production. Production is simply the fruit of proper work habits.

"How many contacts does it take you to get someone to enroll?" It's a question I often ask, and usually the other person hasn't a clue.

"What is your enrollment percentage?" Crickets.

"What is your enrollment to auto-ship percentage?" "What is your PV (person volume) per presentation?" Crickets times two.

Finally, "What rank would you like to achieve in the next 60 days?" Maybe the person isn't sure, but often they'll say, "I'd like to be Gold."

"Do you know how many contacts and presentations you need in order to achieve that rank?" Usually crickets again.

A STARfish doesn't do crickets. Knowing your ratios allows you to predict the activity you need to perform in order to get the result you desire. Otherwise—ever begin a month not knowing how many presentations you need to do? That is pressure!

If your average point value per presentation is 1,000 and you need 3,000 in volume to reach a certain rank, then you will need to do three presentations (minus auto-ship) to hit your goal! So at the beginning of the month you can look at how many presentations you have set and know within a few hundred PV what your volume will be or how many presentations you still need to fill. Knowing up front what action you need to take will let you breathe a lot easier than getting to the end of the month and freaking out. And it's a lot easier to coach your business builders if you know this information before you do a coaching call with them.

The following list of simple activities will help you keep track of your numbers and plan the smaller activities that lead to big results.

SIGNIFICANCE-PRODUCING ACTIVITIES

- Contacts
- Samples given
- Invites
- Presentations scheduled
- Presentations held
- Invites who attended

- Invites who enrolled
- Invites who did auto-ship
- New presentations set from the presentation
- Referrals
- Membership overviews performed
- Business overview/opportunities performed

THE LAW OF AVERAGES

Why wait to get started. Why think about whom you are going to call. Just pick up the phone and make the call or shoot that personal text. Let's say you have three people on your list, and you make the calls, and no one accepts an invitation to your presentation. What do you do? Quit? Never. You learn to fall in love with the law of averages. Remember? Thirty percent of people will always buy from you.

When you focus on performing an activity, you will discover that good things often happen long after a focus on production would have told you to quit. For example . . .

Imagine a neighborhood with 15 houses on each side of the street. Based on the law of averages, there are likely 9 enrollments in those 30 houses. All you have to do is knock. (Yes, I know, you may not share your products door-to-door—at least, not yet! But you get the picture.)

Most people knock on the first few doors, get three noes, and stop. "It doesn't work." "No one wants to buy." "I'm bothering people. I wonder what they will think about me."

Others drive to a coffee shop to *think* about making more calls. Or they listen to one more positive CD or browse a few pages from *The Greatest Salesman in the World* for an attitude boost. What they don't do is keep knocking.

But you're game to try a couple more doors. So what happens when you get to the fifth house and no one has enrolled? Do you keep going and play the law of averages? Or do you go home and wait until you *feel* like making more calls?

Using our example above, perhaps you've already discovered in your business that three enrollments are usually found in the last eight houses. So if you stop when you feel like stopping rather than at a time you've predetermined, you'll never be able to help those last three people who would enroll if you simply showed up.

As you keep going, you gain momentum. Your names start to roll. You gain confidence. And God rewards your perseverance. But you have to be out there.

So embrace the beginning stages of your business. People who want to be an expert right out of the gate end up doing nothing. Their pride is more important than their dreams. Some won't teach a class or do a presentation because they feel they need to know everything before they get started. Trust me, you will never know everything. Others wait for inspiration to hit before they make the call or set up a presentation, not realizing that activity is what breeds passion. This is why so many people are paralyzed by fear. They procrastinate doing the activity that scares them the most, and all it does is turn into a monster that devours their dreams.

Never quit knocking. Never give up on a day, a week, or a month. Good things happen after five o'clock on Friday. Good things happen the last few days of the month. Good things are going to happen behind the next door down. All you have to do is knock.

SERVING PEOPLE

When your heart is on service, you're never nervous. STARfish have a clear picture of what they want to accomplish and whom they can help. They know that action cures all fear and that action or inaction is what determines our feelings.

If you want to feel a certain way, you need to act a certain way. You don't need to read another page in your self-help book, learn another product book, or wait another 15 minutes before you pick up the phone. You will never feel like doing something more than at the moment when you know you should be doing it.

When you focus on serving people, you take the focus off of yourself and put it on them. If you are nervous approaching someone or picking up the phone, it is probably because you're thinking about what *you* want instead of what the customer wants. Concentrate instead on how your product will help them.

Having systems in place, knowing what you're going to say, and focusing on simply doing the next activity, whether it's a contact, a share, a presentation, or an enrollment—these are part of the way you think when you're a STARfish.

The SELLfish, on the other hand, focuses on getting the sale and getting out of there before the customer changes her mind. Since SELLfish rarely follow up, they get few referrals. And because they make so few contacts each day, naturally they feel nervous approaching people—because every contact has got to count. They don't let the law of averages play to their favor. When you commit to making 10 or more contacts per day, then you know that a few of them will want to come to a presentation. But if you are only making one or two, you need every person to attend. That's good old-fashioned sales pressure on you and on your customer.

The STARfish cares about making a difference at every house and with every person, regardless of whether anyone enrolls. When your goal is to deliver value, not make a sale, then the pressure is off of everyone.

Before I do a presentation, I picture myself leaving every person in a better mood than when they arrived. I want some son or daughter to tell their parents, "Wow, that was a really cool person! He was different. I want to be like him." I want parents telling each other how they admire the way I do the job—how I work hard and treat people well regardless of whether they enroll.

I picture people learning about attitude by seeing how positive mine is when someone tells me no. I want my impact on a family to go far beyond the products and my company. When I leave their house after 10:00 P.M., I want the bounce in my step to renew their hope in direct selling and in people in general.

I picture some kid working harder for her dreams because she noticed me working hard for mine. Helping her achieve significance in the future is the Why that drives me.

I know that I can be successful when I redefine what success means to me. It's not about enrollments. When your goal is selling and you fail to sell, you are down. But when you focus on controlling what you can control—your attitude, your schedule, your work habits, and your commitment to serve people for their own sake regardless of the outcome—then success is yours.

Every time.

CHAPTER 7

PRINCIPLE 4:
LEARN HOW PEOPLE BUY

People don't buy what you are selling;
they buy what you get them to say.

—Neal Anderson

STARfish know how people buy and have mastered the process customers go through before they make a buying decision. STARfish know what people like and what they don't like, and as a result, they have cultivated four qualities that SELLfish don't possess.

1. STARFISH KNOW THAT PEOPLE LOVE TO BUY BUT DISLIKE BEING SOLD

Have you ever listened to a sales pitch in which the salesperson did 99 percent of the talking? They were so excited to show you their new widget that they totally forgot the most important factor in sharing successfully: YOU!

One day while I was filling up our Jeep with gas, a guy in a black Suburban pulled up next to me and asked, "Hey, I have an extra home entertainment system. Do you want one?" (Yes, I know—a little strange, but not to a former door-to-door salesman). I replied, "No thank you."

He responded enthusiastically with the old "I can give you a really good deal on it." I politely said no. His determination to find a way to sell his last system of the day at a gas pump was commendable, but he did not understand how people buy. He was sort of a SELLfish.

A STARfish knows that he needs to make it all about the other person, and he seeks to put that person at ease. He builds a sharing environment by reassuring the prospect that it's okay to say no if the product isn't for him. Because the STARfish prioritizes the prospect's well-being, he will leave that person in a good mood regardless of his buying decision.

The STARfish will also ask a lot of questions before talking about the product. Had my salesman in the Suburban been a STARfish, he would have said, "Hey sir, I know this may sound kind of crazy, but I'm the one who has been sitting down with a lot of families here in the North Raleigh area and installing these really cool home entertainment systems. I know you may not be in the market for one, but if you watch a fair amount of TV or movies and would like to get a really good value on a system, would it be worth taking a few minutes to at least check it out? I promise to leave you in a good mood either way."

2. STARFISH ARE IN A HURRY!

Don't you hate it when a salesperson promises it'll "only take a minute" for you to hear their pitch, and then they end up taking an hour! SELLfish rarely ask, "Is this is a good time?" or "I didn't catch you in the middle of something important, did I?" They go right into their pitch regardless of your time or interest.

Not a STARfish. She acknowledges that most people are busy, so she has a sense of urgency, and she lets people know right away. She apologizes for being in a hurry and is honest when she says it will only take a few minutes. This approach increases trust, and it allows her to get to the point quickly and invite people to learn more about her products.

So before someone tells you they don't have time, get there first. Let them know that you regret being so hasty, but you only have a quick minute. And mean it!

3. STARFISH ARE NOT PUSHY

The third reason people dislike SELLfish is because they are pushy. No one likes dealing with a salesperson who pressures them to do something they do not want to do.

I once listened to an audio recording of a conversation between a service representative for a major cable company and a customer who called to cancel his account. The rep would not comply with the gentleman's request. Instead he went on and on, putting pressure on the caller, trying to talk the man out of his express wishes.

Have you ever had the delight of receiving a call during dinner from a telemarketer who tried to keep you on the phone even though you told him you were in the middle of supper with your family? Or walked into a store and found yourself almost instantly telling a little white lie? You know: the first thing the clerk said to you was, "Can I help you?" And you replied, "No, I'm *just looking.*" You experienced pressure, even though the clerk felt she was just helping you.

You do like to buy, though, don't you? Sure you do. Under the right circumstances and given a product you truly desire, it's a pleasure to spend your money on something you know you'll be happy with.

By creating a safe, unpressured sales environment, STARfish help their customers enjoy the process of purchasing products whose value to them is clear and which they know they'll be glad they bought. Buying is fun when you can relax, get helpful information, and freely choose to purchase for the right reasons.

4. STARFISH LEAVE PEOPLE IN A GREAT MOOD

SELLfish are so focused on making the sale that they may unintentionally leave people in a bad mood when the customer says no. They tend to argue with prospects and say things like, "Don't you want to be healthy?" Or they may leave the presentation exasperated because people didn't enroll.

That's not how STARfish operate. They put the interests of others first, and their customers can tell.

When people know that you genuinely care about what's best for them, to the extent that you can graciously take no for an answer, they will appreciate your attitude—and you. You can be someone who makes their day a little better. That's the mark of a STARfish. And remember, what goes around comes around. Sow a blessing and reap its fruit.

FOUR KEYS TO GETTING A DECISION

Before we get into the sales cycle, we need to discuss the big picture it fits in. There are four questions a STARfish knows the answer to by the time she concludes a customer interaction. Those answers will optimize your chances of getting enrollments. So as you read each step of the sales cycle, keep the following in mind:

- Do you know the client's pain?
- Do they have money?
- What is their decision-making process?
- What is the next step?

PAIN

People do not buy features and benefits, contrary to what many in sales are taught. *They buy avoidance of pain and/or a move toward pleasure.* We often miss that point when we talk too much about the products or opportunity. Is there any dissatisfaction going on in the life of your potential customer? Do they love their job, are they healthy, are finances a source of stress? Find out! There are some great questions coming up.

MONEY

You've reached the end of the presentation, and now you hear it: "I don't have the money" or "That's a lot of money!" Frustrating, isn't it. But often it's just an excuse people use to avoid making a decision. After all, most people purchase plenty of things that either are not in their budget or are "too expensive." Consider the average house, car, and toys that may be gathering dust in the garage. We have all purchased things that were "not in our budget" or that we didn't really need.

Of course, it's possible that a person truly is not in a financial position to make a buying decision. So don't get so excited about your product that you fail to qualify your prospect. Does he or she in fact have the money necessary to make the purchase?

Usually, though, the real question is, are they willing to spend their money on what you are offering?

You can begin to address that concern before a presentation gets underway, because it is important to put people at ease regarding any issues with money. One way to do so is to mention that what they are going to see tonight is something everyone can afford. There is something for everyone. And in light of [your value proposition] being so important here in [name of town/city], people are investing in things that can help improve health, decrease costs, and support the family's overall well-being, increase income, freedom etc.

Knowing the budget people have to work with is a key to taking the pressure off your prospects. More times than not, when someone says, "It's not in the budget," they don't even have a budget—and if they do, you can probably create a category in it provided you can demonstrate the need for one.

If something is important enough to someone, they will find the money. Think about this: Many company enrollment kits are priced around $550. A person may tell you he doesn't have that kind of money. But what would happen if someone offered him a brand new Jeep Wrangler on sale for $550? Would he find the money? When people tell you they don't have money, they usually do. You just haven't convinced them that your product is worth the price.

DECISION MAKING PROCESS

Your company sounds great, an attendee tells you, but she needs to talk to her husband, or she wants to think about it.

One way to avoid this objection is to discover who makes the decision (which is usually the mom in many network marketing company offerings) and how that person typically goes about making purchasing decisions. Some people can decide on the spot. Others have to have a family board meeting before spending anything over 25 dollars!

NEXT STEP

"I'll get back to you." "Let me think it over." "The presentation sounds interesting. Call me again after the holidays."

People's responses suggest actions you need to take. Do you always have a next step on the calendar? When you enroll people, do you schedule a membership overview before they leave the presentation?

By asking yourself, "What is the next step?" you will discover up front whether people are simply too nice to say no or are truly interested. Sometimes the next step is the last step because they are not interested. And that is fine.

CREATING A SHARING ENVIRONMENT

How does it feel to deal with a salesperson who instantly puts pressure on you? Think about it for a few seconds. What are some of the things you are thinking? Feeling? Are you excited to be in this conversation? Of course not!

STARfish take the pressure off at the very beginning of any customer interaction, whether it is face-to-face, a phone call, a

Facebook or text message, or a conversation at the beginning of a presentation. They create a sharing environment by letting people know right away that if they like what they see, great, but if not, that is totally okay. STARfish will leave their prospects in a great mood regardless of whether they decide to move forward.

Remember, there is an elephant in the room before any selling situation takes place. The elephant is people's fear barrier. They are thinking, "Will I have to buy anything, and if I don't, will I get out of here alive?" You can help them move past their apprehension by creating a sharing environment. That is likely the number one thing STARfish do to set themselves apart from other salespeople. You can have the highest rank or years of business experience, but if you don't know how to create a sharing environment, then you will likely hear a lot of noes.

You need to give people permission to say no so they will feel comfortable saying yes. The sharing environment takes away most of the pressure. When you contact people or invite them to a presentation, remember that your main goal is serving people and helping them get what they want.

Here is an example of what I will say at the beginning of a presentation to address the Fear Elephant:

> I appreciate everyone's coming tonight. Before we get started, I have a few rules.
>
> First, tonight is going to be entirely about you and helping you learn about some tools and ideas that can help you (insert your company value proposition).
>
> The second rule is this: How many of you have ever been to a home party—you know, where everyone gets together and you hear about a product and then you end up going home with your

twelfth spatula or another handbag? Well, tonight we are going to teach you some things that will change your life, and if you decide that we are a fit for you and your family, then that is great. We will get you set up tonight and you will be on your way to living the lifestyle in a few days.

But if you decide that it's not for you, then it is totally okay to tell me no. One of the things I dislike is being pressured into buying something or feeling like I have to get something simply because I came to a party or presentation. No one likes that.

We are simply passionate about helping people who see us as a fit. And as for those who don't, you will be left in a better mood than when you came, and you will leave with a great education. Does that sound okay? Excellent!

PSYCHOLOGICAL PATH OF THE BUYING PROCESS

STARfish know how to guide people through the buying process, which includes both educating them and motivating them. People do not usually embrace what is best for them without a little education and motivation.

As Terry Weaver writes in his book *The Secrets of Selling from the Masters*, "All buyers must take a mental and emotional journey down that buying path. Everyone receives input from both the right and left sides of the brain. Consequently, your presentation must address both sides to be successful. Your two primary functions are *educating* and *motivating* your prospect."[9]

---

9 Terry Weaver, *The Secrets of Selling from the Masters: Life Lessons and Sales Insights from Real Estate Aces . . . and More* (SECA Press, 2003), 16–17.

Often we do too much educating. We talk about facts and features instead of benefits. We speak to the head instead of the heart. Speaking to the head causes people to think, and that's good, but speaking to the heart causes them to feel—and it's the feeling part that causes people to buy.

Have you ever had someone tell you they "want to think about it"? As Terry describes, thinking causes procrastination while feeling results in action. We need to balance how we share information so we don't do too much educating and not enough motivating.

THE BUYING LINE

STARfish know when people are ready to make a buying decision. They also know that there is a process people must go through in order to be emotionally *and* logically invested in the offer.

So STARfish do not skip steps, and they do not go off-script. They use a duplicable system to ensure that each person gets the information they need in the most efficient way that will allow them to make a decision.

Every product, service, or idea has a *buying line* as well as a best path for guiding people along that buying line and helping them make the best decision in the least amount of time with the least amount of frustration.

The chart on the following page illustrates how the buying line works. Let's apply it to a presentation. As the presentation progresses, interest goes up. The key is to know when people have enough interest to make a decision, and to not waste time once they've reached that point. We do this by asking questions throughout the course of the presentation (or the phone call, or the one-on-one meeting).

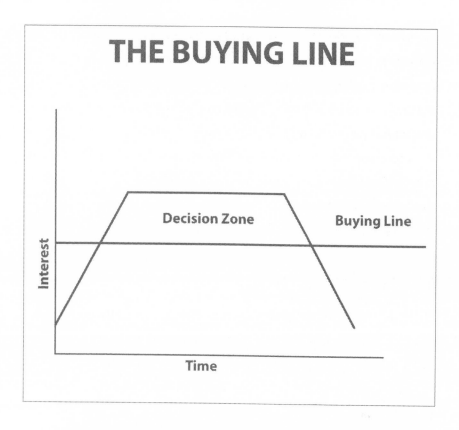

There is another buying line for getting people to a presentation, but you can miss its decision zone if you take too much time talking about the products instead of inviting the person to a presentation. Talk too much and people are likely to become disinterested.

The adult attention span is between eight seconds and 40 minutes. (The average attention span of a goldfish is nine seconds!) So closing the presentation should begin no later than about the 40-minute mark. Unfortunately, SELLfish often talk way past the point at which people are ready to buy. Some people are ready to enroll before the presentation begins! Others are ready halfway through the presentation, still others at the end, and some are never ready—and that's okay.

When I help companies begin to sell a product, service, or idea, I help them focus on what they need to ask, say, and do to help people get to the buying line in the most efficient manner. Often a SELLfish will talk and talk and talk about their product when the customer is already in the decision zone. "I just need to show her one more product to get her to buy," the distributor is telling herself—but the customer is ready to purchase *now*! Ultimately the sale is lost because the buyer becomes frustrated. And we all know that a frustrated buyer does not buy.

STARfish understand that people don't necessarily buy products—*they buy ideas that will solve their problems*. Perhaps you've heard the story about the guy who walks into a hardware store and asks the clerk to recommend a good drill. The clerk goes on and on about all the features of every drill in the store. Finally, after about 15 minutes, the man gets frustrated. "Son, I appreciate your taking the time to explain each of these drills," he says to the clerk, "but I didn't come here today because I want to buy a drill. I want a hole!"

How many times do we make our presentation all about our product and fail to help people find the "hole" they are really looking for. For my customers, that would be better health, improved mental performance, smoother skin, and other benefits that our products can provide. What about your customers? What is the hole your product or service can help them drill?

CHAPTER 8

PRINCIPLE 5: MASTER THE SALES FUNDAMENTALS: THE SALES CYCLE

Unless you have deliberately formed the habit
of calling on prospects to make them see their reasons
for buying your product, then unconsciously you have
formed the habit of calling on prospects in a state
of mind in which you are willing to let them
make you see their reasons for not buying it.

—Albert E. N. Gray

Mastering the simple sales fundamentals will make all the difference between an average career in network marketing and a great one. Have you wondered if there is a better way to assist people along the path from prospective customer to enrollee? Do you struggle to get your team up to speed quickly? Have you ever reached the end of a presentation and heard the old "Let me talk to my husband" or "Let me think about it"? Do you ever feel pressure when you invite people to a presentation?

Chapter 7 addresses these and other concerns by taking you through the sales cycle. This is easily the longest chapter in the book, with insights that can make a dramatic difference in your journey.

The sales cycle is a system that provides a common language for the process people go through from having never heard about your company to enrolling and providing you with referrals to friends and family who would love to hear about what you do and why you do it. When you can break down the process into individual steps and then, over time, master each step, you drastically increase your enrollment percentage and ultimately duplicate more quickly. When you understand the psychology behind each fundamental, then you can teach it to others.

We'll cover some of the steps quickly. Others, we'll spend time covering in depth. Each of them is vital to your success.

THE SALES CYCLE

We'll begin our discussion of the sales cycle itself by getting an overview. The chart on the next page gives you a graphic illustration of the order of the cycle.

Beginning with "Connect" and proceeding clockwise, you progress through 11 key steps, concluding with "Referrals" and "Follow-up." In actual practice, since you're normally working with a number of people at the same time, you may find yourself running multiple sales cycles and dealing with a different step in each of those cycles. The order of steps for every person is always the same; however, some people may spend less time than others in one step or another. Let's take a closer look at each of those steps.

CONNECT

"It is easier to sell to people who don't want [your product] than it is to find people who do want it," said sales sage Albert E. N. Gray.[10] But, he continued, if you have not deliberately formed the habit of prospecting for *needs*, not just wants, then you limit your

---

10 Albert E. N. Gray, "The Common Denominator of Success," in a PDF on Amnesta.com, accessed May 9, 2017, http://www.amnesta.net/mba/thecommonde-nominatorofsuccess-albertengray.pdf.

prospecting—because many people who need what you've got won't immediately want it. They may not know they need it. You've got to help them understand why they do.

The Connect step involves simply finding the ideal customer for what you have. The key is to have as many poles in the water as possible so you can have an endless supply of new people to help. Fortunately for many network marketing businesses, pretty much everyone is a potential prospect.

The first part of Connecting is to develop a list of people with whom you can share. The larger your list, the less pressure you will feel. It's amazing how many people come out of the woodwork when you go through Facebook friends, LinkedIn, church directories, neighbors, friends, and family. Networking groups are another way to increase exposure, but be careful that you do not attend just to sell your stuff! Networking is about building relationships, and that takes time.

Sharing your business online is a hot topic that we will save for another day. However, you should know this much: Sharing online may work, but it is difficult to duplicate. At an online leadership summit where Randy Gage and I were presenters, Randy pointed out that if Bill Gates were to sign up with your company and incorporate your presentation into the next version of Windows so it would pop up on all the computers worldwide . . . that could work. Bill would get new enrollments. But would others be able duplicate what he did? Not unless they owned a multibillion-dollar company that had access to computers screens all over the world.

If you are going to use the Internet to build your business, you have still got to get your arms around the principles and systems in this book. Otherwise, your future success online will be greatly diminished, and you'll risk gaining the SELLfish reputation that is so common in our profession.

The second part of Connecting is to find out everything you can about the person you plan to call. By familiarizing yourself with your prospects before you call them, you'll build trust and credibility more quickly.

LinkedIn is a great way not only to connect but also to learn critical information about people so you can find a common bond. For example, before you call a chiropractor, look her up in LinkedIn and see which of your connections might know her. You can then call that person and ask them to tell you a little bit about the chiropractor. Often your connection will call the chiropractor or write an email connecting the two of you. LinkedIn is an unlimited list of leads and intelligence, and Facebook can be beneficial as well so long as it does not consume your life!

CONTACT

Your success and significance in life will be in direct proportion to the number of times you put yourself and others in a position to say yes or no.

There are only four possible results when you contact someone, so don't freak out!

You may get a yes.

You may get a no.

You may get a no with a life lesson.

Or you may be met with procrastination.

Any of these results in itself is no big deal. So why is it such an issue for us to pick up the phone and invite a friend to a presentation?

What goes through our heads just before we do? Are we excited—or hoping they don't answer our call? I know how it goes. I've been there and I'm still there. But it gets easier the better we get.

To be successful, we need to take the emotion out of making the contact. The worst that can happen is that someone says no.

Yes is a great answer. But no is a great answer too. And no with a life lesson is a great answer. Only procrastination can sap the life out of us. It leaves us with a false hope that the person will come to a presentation or enroll or call us back when they ask for our card. But in reality, procrastination is often just a way people disguise their "No" because they're too nice to refuse us directly.

So how will you handle procrastination? Buy into the person's inaction—or turn them around? Which will prevail—their reason for not taking action, or the benefit you show them that overrides their reluctance and spurs them to act?

FOUR STAGES OF INTEREST

We often feel pressure in the contacting phase because we focus on the end result instead of the next step. We do the other person no good by mentally jumping them ahead of where they're actually at. So it's essential to recognize the four stages of interest people move through when they become customers in your business.

1. In the *learning stage*, you seek people who are *open* to learning about what you do. This is where people come to a presentation or a one-on-one meeting or perhaps attend a webinar. The question here is, "Are you open to learning about XYZ?" From there, we simply ask people if they are open to using our product or service.

2. The *living stage* is where people become a "product of the product." By actually using and experimenting with the various products, they gain firsthand knowledge.

3. Once someone is experienced with the product or service, they're ready to leave their comfort zone and move on to the *sharing stage*. Much like how they want to tell their friends about a great dining experience or a movie they enjoyed, people who use your products want to share the benefits with those around them. The question here is, "Are you open to teaching others" or "Are you open to creating an income with (your company)."

4. Finally, in the *building stage*, people are actively growing their own business, training their team, and attempting to supplement or replace their income. This fourth stage is where duplication is the key.

The pressure people often feel in network marketing, and sales in general, comes from trying to put people in stage two, three, or four too quickly. This is one of the main reasons why so many people are averse to network marketers.

Some of the companies in our profession lead with the opportunity. You know—they call you up and tell you about a great new chance to live the dream, or make a lot of money, or win a car. Not only is this approach unprofessional but it ignores the natural progression people go through when building belief in a product or cause.

People naturally want to first learn something about the products and the company. Then they want a chance to experience the products or services before committing to build a new business. Yes, some companies have been built on selling the opportunity and promoting the dream lifestyle. But this approach makes getting an audience much more difficult. It's a lot easier to go after the 97 percent of people who are not network markers!

It's foolish to attempt selling the dream before the person trusts the dreamer. Yet it happens every day, and every day another person becomes disenchanted with network marketing. Every day another saleswoman feels scared to pick up the phone because she's supposed to talk her prospect into doing something that person knows zero about.

STARfish have a much better way: understanding how to serve people where they are instead of luring them prematurely down a glowing path with promises of fancy cars and the dream lifestyle. Those things will come—but only after they put in the hard work.

COMMUNICATION 101

Perhaps you've heard that communication is 7 percent word; 38 percent tone, rate, and volume; and 55 percent body language. Most people will evaluate the emotional aspects of your message not by the words you use but by your nonverbal cues and signals. It is critical that you do three things to ensure you communicate the right message.

Slow down and speak in a low voice. It's easy to get nervous when you contact someone. You know the feeling: your voice rises in pitch and you speak faster than you usually do. Have you ever experienced a nervous telemarketer? He didn't sound normal, did he? He spoke so fast that you couldn't understand him—because he knew that if he kept talking, you couldn't interrupt him with an "I'm not interested." Don't you be that way. Just monitor your speaking voice, that's all.

Watch your body language. Are you moving back and forth? Are your body actions inconsistent with your words? Do you wave your hands around, shift your eyes, or change positions often? These behaviors all convey nervousness, not confidence.

People are *feeling* what you are saying more than they are paying attention to your actual words. They get distracted by out-of-sync body gestures, lack of eye contact, and too many filler words such as "um" and "you know."

Finally, remember: people think seven times faster than you talk. You can be in the middle of mentioning the benefits of your product or opportunity in a grocery line and your prospect is already thinking, "I like this. It sounds pretty cool! How do I get it?" So be sensitive to where they're at. Don't go on and on about features and benefits when you should be inviting the person to come to your next event!

FIVE WAYS TO CONTACT PEOPLE

There are five main ways you can contact people:
1. Face-to-face
2. Phone
3. Text/instant message
4. Invitation
5. Facebook/social media post

The best way to contact someone is of course face-to-face. It's a lot more difficult to tell someone no to his or her face. In fact, it is often harder for a prospect to say no than for us to hear it! You also have the ability to cover concerns they may have that you would not discover through a text or social media.

Remember the Connect stage? Make sure you have completed it before you initiate a contact so you have useful information about the person you're contacting. And remember why people don't like salespersons: They are pushy. They leave people in a bad mood. They take up too much time. And they fail to understand people's needs.

You want to create a sense of urgency by apologizing up front to those you contact for being in a big hurry. You're sorry—you only have a quick second. This lets people know that your interaction won't take all day. And adopt a mindset much like the one you'd have if you were inviting people to a Superbowl party or over to dinner. You want them to come because of the value they will receive by hanging out with some cool people watching the Superbowl or enjoying a home-cooked meal. When we contact our friends, we usually do not take it personally if they do not come. We just call them the next time.

Think of a waitress checking tables to ask who wants a coffee refill. Does she skip a table for fear of being told no? Does she even care what answer she may get? No. The waitress simply goes to every table with a great attitude and asks each person, "Would you like a refill?" She doesn't get overexcited when people say yes or down when people say no; her job is simply to give diners the option, fill the cups of those who say yes, and pass the ones who say no.

How about you? Some will tell you yes and others will say no. Your job is simply to ask people if they are open to what you are offering. For those who say yes, teach them. For those that say no, simply move on. Talk to your company leaders to get the scripts they use to contact people, and duplicate those scripts in your team.

How many people are you going to contact, and who are they? You should know that before you proceed. Have a list of 20 to 30 names sitting on your desk before you start making calls. We all know how hard it is to make calls flying by the seat of our pants. And calling a bunch of people at one time lets you leverage the momentum.

Your job is not to sell people. Your job is to make a list and then cross people off it one by one. Some people will want to come to a presentation; some will not. Some will procrastinate; others will say they are coming but they never show up. So memorize this little saying and rehearse it in your head:

Some will. Some won't. So what! Who's next?

Again, your job is simply to make a list and then cross people off it. You need contacts, presentations, and enrollments to have a good week. Who's next . . . and next . . . and next . . . ?

ANSWER A QUESTION WITH A QUESTION

The person you're talking with has just asked you The Question: "What do you do?" What do you tell her?

A million ideas flood your head—too many. What was that clever line a colleague used? You can't remember; your brain is frozen. You could just say, "I sell essential oils"—but what if the person is allergic to the scent? Then you've ruined an opportunity. It wouldn't be the first time.

Remember this timeless principle: Answer a question with a question. First, learn why the person is asking. Usually there is a reason, and once you discover it, you can customize your answer to fit your prospect's situation. That approach has far more potential than simply answering the person's question directly and getting an unpleasant surprise. That's how to lose a perfectly good customer.

Back in my real estate days, I heard a story about a husband and wife who were looking for vacation property in South Carolina. The wife asked whether the community had a golf course. The salesman replied enthusiastically that it did—and promptly discovered that a golf course isn't always a selling point. The wife didn't want to live in a community with a golf course because she would never see her husband!

A STARfish would have told the wife that it was a great question and then inquired why she asked. Once the wife informed him about her husband's golf habit, the salesperson could have asked her other questions to discover her interests. He might have found that she would enjoy a day at the spa or fellowship with the other ladies at the club while her husband played golf. Or he could have explained to her that ownership in a community with a golf course would be a major benefit for increasing the property value, as many people seek a community with a golf course, especially in Hilton Head, South Carolina.

You should always answer the question "What do you do?" with a question, especially at networking events. For instance:

> It really depends. Sometimes I'm changing diapers, and other times I'm playing referee; sometimes I'm fixing boo-boos, and other times I'm traveling. By the way—what do *you* do?

Get them talking about themselves first and try to deflect the question back to them. Ask great questions, and then they will become genuinely interested in what you do. Then you can begin asking "do you know how" questions. For instance, as a health and wellness advocate, you might say something like this:

> Do you know how a ton of people these days are looking for natural alternatives? You know—because most products have toxicity and are bad for your skin? I was talking with one person the other day, and she couldn't believe some of those things are still legal to sell!

So, what I do is work with doctors, nurses, chiropractors, professional athletes, families, and folks just like us, and I teach them how to use natural alternatives that end up being safer, cheaper, and more effective forms of wellness. Are you like most people and into that type of stuff? Why is it so important to you? Everyone seems to have a different answer.

Wait for them to respond and then say,

That is exactly why everyone is so excited to come to a class/workshop/presentation. I have a few on the schedule. Pull out your calendar and let's get you plugged in.

SHARE

Your company may have a process in which you share a sample of the product or give a DVD to help people become more familiar with what you do. However, the better you become at the sales cycle, the less often you will need to provide a product experience, sample, or DVD

Sharing a sample or DVD can often prolong the sales cycle if you do not invite the person to a presentation, or if you try to teach them too much too fast and then fail to close on setting an appointment. The best scenario is simply inviting them to a presentation or setting a one-on-one appointment so they can sample *all* of your products at the same time! The personal appointment or presentation gives you the best chance to get a decision, because people get all of the important information and value proposition at once. The absolute best sample is at your house on a Tuesday or Thursday evening at 7pm where they can *sample* whatever they want!

Nevertheless, sharing may be a part of your company's cycle, because some people need a few experiences before they enroll. Talk to your leader to find out the best practice in your company.

If sharing is part of your sales cycle, don't leave the house without your products/samples! Even if sharing is *not* part of your cycle, you should keep your products on hand. Think of how often you've overheard someone complaining about a problem your product could solve, and you kicked yourself because you didn't have any samples.

Sharing begins with focusing 100 percent on helping the other person get the help they need right in the moment. Give the person a small experience (if your products can be sampled) and then ask, "What's the best way to contact you? I'll follow up with you in a few days to see how you are doing."

Your confidence will be that person's confidence, and if your heart is in the right place—that is, you really care about helping your prospective customer—then you will eventually have a new fan!

INVITE

Step 4 is really the second part of contacting people, and it often occurs without your having to share a sample. The Invite step, in which you ask people to attend a presentation or or a one-on-one, is another opportunity to get a yes or a no. So naturally, it's also another opportunity to confront fear.

We feel uneasy about inviting someone to a presentation or one-on-one. Instead, we keep talking. Why?

We procrastinate because of fear. Fear that we will get a no. Fear that someone might say, "Is it network marketing?" Or, "Give me your card and I'll get back to you." Or, "How much are they?"

I've observed people doing what amounted to a mini-presentation, going through many of their products or promoting their opportunity instead of simply asking the person, "Based on what you just told me about your (fill in the blank), you seem like a perfect fit to visit one of my classes. I have one next Tuesday evening at 6:30 and one Thursday at 7:00. Which one would best fit your schedule—or would it be better for us to visit one-on-one this week?"

Have you ever had a great conversation with someone who seemed interested, but you did not have a presentation on the schedule to invite them to? This is a big reason why people have low invites. Make sure you have at least two presentations on the schedule at all times so people can have an option. When you have something to invite people to, it's a lot easier to ask!

EXPLORE

The brownies are hot. The snacks are yummy. The people are arriving—and you are excited! You get everyone a few refreshments and jump right into talking about your company, products, or opportunity.

Too bad. You've just skipped over the step where 80 percent of all enrollment decisions occur—the Explore stage.

You have probably heard many times that your products sell themselves. That may be partly true—your products may have built-in appeal; however, if you think that merely offering a sample will make a credit card automatically appear, you might want to take a step back for a moment. There is a lot more going on behind the scenes. And that is why the Explore stage is vital and why you should never leapfrog over it and immediately start passing around products or talking about your opportunity.

"Neal, that is crazy," you say. "These are the best products in the world. We are simply an awesome company. All I need to do is let people experience the product or learn about our opportunity, and sales and enrollments will be a breeze."

I only wish it were that easy. If this is your method of sharing and it works for you, awesome. However, why not invest a little more time to help the remaining 80 percent of people who might have enrolled had you gone through the Explore step before introducing the products.

People buy the *problem* before they buy the product. And then they don't really buy the product—they buy the feeling they get when they use the product. They buy how painful their headache is and how good it feels to get relief. They buy how burned out they feel after three sleepless nights and how wonderful it is to finally wake up refreshed. They buy how good their skin looks and feels at long last after years of exposure to the sun. They buy the slim waistline that allows them to put on the bikini without feeling self-conscious.

That's the level we've got to speak on. If we don't, we will lose good customers and potential business builders.

The Explore step is the emotional part of the presentation. It's where decisions are made—because, remember, while people justify their purchases with their logic, they make them with their emotions. So when the emotional step gets skipped, is it any wonder that enrollment percentages drop, or that at the end of the presentation you hear, "I want to think about it" and "Let me talk to my spouse."

There's yet another reason why this stage is so critical: it's the stage where customer objections get answered before they even arise.

In sales interaction, the first person to the objection wins. So cover the most common objections in your presentation *before* you talk about the products or service. For example, if you forget to talk about the purity, the sourcing, and the testing that makes your essential oils far superior to what people can get in the store, don't be surprised at the end of the presentation to hear, "I can get those at the store for half the price." No, they can't—not anything like the quality you offer. But it's a lot more effective to convince people of that up front. Ditto the objection "I'm not comfortable enrolling until I talk to my doctor." You can easily defuse it at the beginning of the presentation by saying that "many doctors not only use my products but also recommend them to their patients." (Of course, you've verified that this is true.)

Then follow up with a question: "Why do you feel so many doctors recommend these products to their patients these days?" The answer people give will likely be a reason they gain confidence in my company. *Never tell someone something you can get them to say for themselves.* Their own answer is more believable to them, and once they've said it, they will own it. Remember, people don't usually buy what you are selling; they buy what you can get them to say. Get them talking by mastering the art of asking questions.

Addressing customer challenges up front not only corrects people's faulty notions but also decreases people's fear of making a decision by having conflicting information in their heads.

QUESTIONS ARE THE ANSWER

We need to master the art of asking questions in order to discover what is important to people. That discovery in turn helps us create an internal need for the products. Questions open people up to buying what we have.

My first professional sales experience was at a house outside of Asheville, North Carolina, talking with a mom about some books that would help her with her kids. The manager I was with had me do the demonstration, and instead of asking questions, I immediately pulled out a book and started explaining the pages.

I kept talking and talking about the product, hoping that by doing so I could keep the customer from saying no. Finally, after the manager hit me in the arm several times with the order pad, I realized that the mom was ready to buy!

The point here is not that many people simply want to buy stuff from us but that if we ask questions and discover what is important to the other person, then we know what to show. And we also know when we need to stop showing and begin signing people up!

CREATING A NEED

Many trainers discuss the importance of a product's features and benefits. You need to talk more about the benefits to people, they tell you—and it's true. Ultimately, people buy to alleviate pain (or create pleasure, to some extent). So if you fail to clearly understand their pain (and their goals), you'll have a hard time getting them to part with their hard-earned money.

You have to create a need and reveal people's dissatisfaction with their current situation. I often tell people in my coaching and training courses, "Good sales people can find a need. Great salespeople can uncover needs. But STARfish *create* needs!"

Your success and significance are determined by many things. One of them is your ability to create a need. In direct selling, we are often introducing a product or service that the customer is not currently using. Because we are bringing it to them for the first time, we need to bear in mind that the customer does not know anything about the product and how it can benefit them.

Granted, it's good to talk about the benefit of using lavender essential oil to support sleep. But that's just scratching the surface. If we don't help the customer understand the implications of sleep loss, a need will not be created, and hence an enrollment is less likely to occur.

The iPad is a hugely successful example of need creation. Before Apple came out with the iPad, how many of us were walking around saying, "I sure wish someone would invent a screen that didn't have a keyboard and a hinge. I can't get through life without one."

One person did come up with such a device. Steve Jobs understood that he could greatly improve the profitability of Apple by creating products that people were not aware they needed until *after* they were introduced to Apple's marketing plan and to the frenzy created by the early adopters who lined up to get the new device.

No one initially needed an iPad. Yet once it was introduced, Apple sold millions of them. That's because the existence of the iPad and what it could do for people created the need for it, and to such a degree that those who already had perfectly good iPads would wait for days in line to get the newest version. *That* is creating a need! Apple understood what was important to people.

Questions open people up, and they also take the focus off of us. If you ever feel nervous about what you are going to say, simply ask a question. People would rather hear what they have to say than what you've got to say!

What kinds of questions should you ask? Let the following ones serve as your guideline. When you know the answers to them *before* you begin talking about the products, your confidence will increase.

And pressure will decrease, because people usually do not buy until they perceive a need. Asking good questions can help you create that need. Here is what you need to know before you begin talking about your product or opportunity:

- What is the person's reality? (Where are they now?)
- What are their goals? (Where do they want to go?)
- What would they change?
- Why would change be important?
- Are you talking to the decision maker(s)?
- Ask the vision question:

  "If you could have more of what you want (health, energy, fitness, time) and less of what you don't want (fat, pain, toxins, expensive medical bills, no time), is that something you would want to…
  - check out?" (if contacting or inviting)
  - use?" (if in a presentation)

Knowing the answers to these six questions will quadruple the number of people who enroll at your presentations or one-on-ones, because now you know what matters most to them. All your product or opportunity does is fill the gap between where they are and where they want to be. That's how simple selling can be!

Ever ask yourself during a presentation, "What is going on in their heads? Are they even interested?" Do you know their goals, concerns, and issues, and why change could be important to your attendees?

In many network marketing companies, moms are the primary customer, and usually they are the decision maker when it comes to the products. Sometimes, though, when a woman says she has to talk to her spouse, she really does. She won't make a financial decision on her own.

Had you known that both parties needed to be part of the decision to enroll, you could have invited the spouse to the presentation or one–on–one. But many times we don't learn about this part of the equation until after the fact. So we need to assure attendees up front that the decision to enroll is one that most wives feel comfortable making because most of the husbands tell them it's their department.

Think about it. When the kids get a boo-boo, to whom do they run? Take it from me, it's usually *not* Dad. When women want to choose a face cream, do they ask their husband's advice?

Once, taking an informal poll, I asked some ladies, "If you want a pair of shoes, do you go home and consult your husband?" Nine out of ten said they didn't even tell their husbands, and the other one hid the shoes in her closet and pulled them out at the appropriate time when her husband was in a good mood!

Of course we don't want spouses to keep secrets about purchases, but we do need to get the facts on the table. In most instances, the wife *can* make the decision, and the husband is brought in simply as an easy way to tell the hostess they are not interested . . . yet!

When you help people create a vision for what could be, you have a solid chance for them to buy into your vision. When you know where they are and where they want to go and then paint that picture in their minds, they develop confidence: "So if you could get in better shape and have more energy, is that something you would want to check out?"

One of the ways to create a need is to have people go through an analysis of the top reasons why someone would buy your product; that process allows them to evaluate their own circumstances. For example, in my business, a Wellness Triangle lists the foundations of optimal health: eating right, exercise, sleep, reducing toxic product use, and so on. Asking people to score themselves on a scale of 1 to 10 in each of the areas immediately creates a little pain for them (it did for me the first time I did it!). That discomfort sparks discussion, and I can then begin to ask some questions:

- Why do you feel so many people are into natural products these days?
- Why would it be important to score above an 8 or 9 on all levels of the Wellness Triangle?
- How would you feel if you could move your scores up a few numbers?
- What do you feel will happen if you don't reach your wellness goals?

Consider what questions would be relevant for *your* clients. And remember, the answers are inside them. You simply need to ask the right questions, and be willing to listen and process the answers.

Notice, by the way, how I used the word *feel* rather than *think* in three of the four questions. Again, people buy out of their emotions, not their intellect. Questions are a great opportunity to engage people on the emotional level.

EDUCATE

Now comes the fun part. You get to finally talk about your products or opportunity! As mentioned earlier, approximately 80 percent of the buying decision has been made by this point in the presentation. Teaching is simply demonstrating how your product or opportunity will solve people's problems. This is the part in which you educate and motivate people to do what is best for themselves.

NOTE: The following is a walk-through using an essential oil product. Your own product line may be quite different from mine. That's okay; the principles are universal. You'll just need to do some extrapolating. Simply follow along with the steps; plug in your product, value proposition, or opportunity in place of mine; and modify the process as you need to.

Begin by understanding the big-picture needs your product line addresses. For essential oil and health products, chances are good that you will be teaching a class in which you share your story, talk about the current state of our healthcare system, and discuss the four main reasons why so many people have been excited to have your products.

One of the traps presenters often fall into is to describe products solely by the way they are used: "This is Peppermint; people use it for head tension or when they are hot. This is Lavender; you use it to support healthy sleep."

That's intriguing to an extent, but there's a more effective way. Here is a little system that will help you build interest, create in people a dissatisfaction with where they're at, and speak to the emotional part of the brain (as discussed in chapter 7).

ATTS

A—Ask a question.
T—"Tell me about that."
T—Tell a third-person story.
S—Show an product/solution.

Here is an example from an essential oil business of how this system could play out in a presentation. Where you need to, simply substitute your own product or service and one of the value propositions.

ASK A QUESTION

First, ask, "How many people have ever had trouble going to sleep or known someone who did?"

Notice how I added "or known someone who did." Here you don't want to ask a question to which you don't know the answer. If you ask only the first part, it is possible that no one will have had that issue, and then you're stuck. But everyone these days knows at least *someone* who has sleeping issues.

"TELL ME ABOUT THAT"

When you get the answer, resist the temptation to jump directly into talking about the solution. Give people a chance to stew for a bit in their dissatisfaction in order to create a need. Remember, people don't buy the product until they buy that there is a problem.

By saying "Tell me about that," you can take people back to the exact time when they tossed and turned and couldn't fall asleep. Keep asking questions such as "How did that affect you the next day? And then what happened?" You want them to vividly recall, in the presentation, how frustrated they felt when they were tossing and turning in their bed two nights ago—because that frustration and the burnout of sleep deprivation are the things they want to, and *can*, change.

TELL A THIRD-PERSON STORY

Next you share an anecdote. Third-person stories are powerful for a couple reasons. First, people believe 25 percent of what you say, but they believe 75 percent of what you can get *them or others to* say. Second, telling the story of someone else who had the problem under discussion, and who found its solution by using the product, will increase confidence and help ease the fear of making a buying decision.

Picture yourself in a grocery store, trying to choose between different breakfast cereals. You are comparing the ingredients, the cost per ounce—and then someone standing beside you says, "My kids love that cereal." What do you do?

Exactly. You put that cereal in the cart. The helpful shopper helped you decide *and* took most of the risk out of making the decision (because now you can blame someone else if the kids don't like it!).

Gather as many third-person stories as you can. You should have a third-person story for every possible customer challenge (objection) and for most of the products you will show in a presentation. As you progress in your business, you will want to have a story for every product.

Here is how telling a third-person story might work. Someone has just told you about their unhealthy sleep cycles. In response, you say, "That's what Erin told me just the other day. She said, 'I have trouble sleeping, and it seems to affect the rest of my day if not the rest of my week. . . .'"

SHOW THE PRODUCT/SOLUTION

Now it's time to introduce the solution: "And that is why Erin loves using Lavender before bedtime. She puts it on the bottom of her feet and even diffuses it. That's another reason she made sure she got the diffuser—so she could support healthy sleep cycles *topically* as well as *aromatically*."

Then you want to ask another question, such as, "Makes sense, doesn't it?" or "Can you see why she was excited to have these products in her home?"

Third-person stories are powerful and should be used in every step of the sales cycle, from contacting through follow-up.

IT'S A DIALOGUE, NOT A MONOLOGUE

Have you ever felt like you were doing all the talking in a presentation? An hour of monologue can be uncomfortable not only for us but for our guests as well.

Asking questions throughout the presentation not only creates a dialogue but also helps us know where people are on the buying line. For example, when we ask, "Makes sense, doesn't it?" we are taking people's temperature so we can see who is with us and who might be daydreaming. Here are some questions you can use:

"What do you feel you would use the most so far, Judy?"

"Sally, what has been your favorite part of the class/workshop so far?"

"Can you begin to see why so many people are now using this with their families?"

"How would you use this at home with *your* kids?"

"How do you see that using this product in your home can benefit your family."

After receiving the answer to a question, you can simply say, "That is what most people have been telling me—and I feel it is why so many people have been excited to use this stuff. One mom said, 'It just makes logical sense to have this around the house.'"

The answers your attendees provide can be used by you during the enrollment step to remind them of the importance of having the products in their home!

10 TIPS FOR TEACHING WITH INSPIRATION

1. Take control.
2. Follow a script.
3. Always speak to a set of eyes
4. Move with purpose.
5. Use voice inflection. Avoid monotone.
6. Focus on body language and eliminate distractions.
7. Follow the A.T.T.S. formula.
8. Use people's names.
9. Avoid *ums* and useless words.
10. Record your presentation so you can get better

SUMMARIZE

After sitting through a presentation, people often forget what you covered in the presentation. Imagine how another person feels trying to digest in 45 minutes information that took you a month to understand!

So it's vital that you summarize the content, including any aha! moments during the presentation. Then begin to ask some opening (the old-school term is *closing*) questions.

The following questions help people focus on the important points they may have gleaned from the presentation. They also help you take the attendee's temperature before you ask them to make an enrollment decision. You can customize these questions to fit your company.

What did you like best about the class/workshop? Was it when we talked about saving money? Or about how you would have safer, more effective options right at home?

Why do you feel your husbands would be so excited to get these in your homes: because it would save your family money in the long run, or because the products would help support health goals—or both?

If you were 100 percent sure, beyond a shadow of a doubt, that you would experience one of your health challenges within the next month, and you already had these products in your home, how would you feel?

(You will see that last question in the next section as well.)

CLOSE

For many people, *closing* is a dirty word. So we will use the term *open*. Open people up to getting some really great products. Open them up to a future revenue stream. Open them up to making a decision that is best for them.

What comes to your mind when you think about the word *closing*? Do you start to get cold sweats? Are you thinking about the last time you purchased a new or used car? No one likes to be pressure-closed. However, people *need* someone to help them make a decision. That is our job as STARfish!

If we are doing our part correctly, we will be viewed as the expert. This is one of the main differences between the direct-selling model and the retail environment: In order for a sale to occur, direct selling requires well-informed consultants to educate the customer about the product. People need to understand our product before they will buy it.

So we in turn must understand the challenges that people go through when making a buying decision. Our job as STARfish is to help people process the education they receive in a presentation and ultimately make a decision that is best for themselves and their families. We need to help them get a vision of their need, because they may not see it unassisted. Most people cannot do these things on their own. Otherwise, they would simply go to a retail store.

Making decisions can be scary! People do not want to make the wrong decision, so they make no decision at all. We do them a service by helping them get past their sticking point to make the decision that is best for them. If you have ever struggled with a decision and then had someone help you through it, you know what I mean.

Our goal is not to pressure people into getting what we have so we can get an enrollment, win some trip, or advance in rank. Save that for the SELLfish. However, be aware that chemical and biological changes occur in people when they are in a decision making mode, and these are enhanced when they perceive that we are there expecting an answer. STARfish seek to help people get past the physiological barriers that can hamper their ability to make wise choices. You may not think of it in those terms, and you don't need to, but it's part of what occurs during a well-conducted close.

So remember: Closing is not something you do *to* people; it's something you do *for* people. Closing is simply the step in the sales cycle where it's time for people to make a decision and then move on. Closing is opening people to the possibilities of having your products or opportunity in their homes.

In fact, *not* closing is more pressure. Think about it. When someone leaves your presentation after telling you they want to "think about it," now you have to call them back: "Hey, it's Neal, and I'm just calling to see if you made a decision." That is pressure!

Or they "need to go home and talk to their husband" when in fact they could have made the decision on their own had we handled their concern in the presentation. Now we have to play telephone tag to get their answer. Have you ever had someone go into the witness protection program to avoid returning your calls?

Closing is not one question but rather a sequence of questions. Think of it as a series of green lights. You ask a question like, "Can you see how using Peppermint could have helped a few times last week?" and wait for the response. If it's yes, then you can go on with the process. If it's no, then you know you have some work to do.

Closing is actually a lot of fun if you know how to do it correctly. Unfortunately, most people do not close correctly and end up putting more pressure on people than if they simply did it the right way. Many people avoid this stage like the plague because they don't want to come off as pushy. So here is a question: Would you feel bummed out if someone had not shared your products or opportunity with you? Exactly! Now pass on the favor by doing everything you can to help others have the same best shot at enrolling. That includes helping them make decisions.

Picture someone sitting on the couch shuffling paperwork. To you they may appear focused and decisive, but in reality they are calling out for help. They are saying "I don't know what I need or what I want. This is all new to me. I need someone with experience to help me decide what to do." People usually do not close themselves. Yet at the end of the presentation, many distributors say something like, "Let me know if you have any questions, and feel free to grab some more refreshments." We think people will automatically fill out the form. I wish it were that easy.

Don't buy the lie that doing anything more than volunteering to answer questions is being pushy. In reality, not sitting down with them and helping them make a decision creates more pressure. People have a difficult time making decisions without your assistance.

You can feel the quiet in the room when a person is making a decision. You feel the pressure as you watch them shuffle their materials and order form. Here are a some questions you can ask to help them along.

> If you were 100 percent sure, beyond a shadow of a doubt, that you would experience one of your (hot buttons/pain points) within the next month, and you already had these products in your home, would you use them? How would you feel if they helped?

> If this could easily fit in your budget and not take food off your table, would there be anything that would prevent you from getting started tonight?

> If you had access to safer, cheaper, and more effective wellness options in your home, would you use them? How would they help your family?

Now you are ready to help people decide if what they just experienced is for them.

SHARE AN EMOTIONAL STORY

Emotional stories help take people from the technical part of the presentation to the emotional aspect of making a decision. If you ever hear "I want to think about it" at the end of a presentation or one-on-one, then you were likely talking to that person's logical part of their brain, and as a result, she is now finding it difficult to make a decision. That's why an emotional story is a vital tool for priming the decision making process.

Here is an example of a third-person, emotional story, told in a way that can help people focus on what is really important and why they would want to enroll. After reading it, write your own third-party story.

> As Jessica said, insurance is expensive to purchase but even more expensive to use. You have copays, out-of-pocket deductibles, and premiums. So while a lot of people think these products might be expensive, they actually fit into everyone's budget.
>
> It's like Suzie told me the other night: "We spend more money on things for the kids, video games, eating out, toys, and cell phone charges, so it made perfect sense to have something like this around the house when we need it!" Plus, she felt she could save a bundle on future medical costs by promoting a healthy lifestyle. That's why she wanted to enroll.

THREE CATEGORIES

Because your company is unique, you should check with your company leaders for advice on how you wrap up your presentation. However, most companies have one thing in common: there are three groups who attend their presentations. One wants to buy. The second thinks they want to buy, but they have questions. Third is the group who are not interested—but if you use the following script, which speaks to all three groups, you may be able to get them interested as they see people start filling out the order forms.

Don't try to meet with every person individually. Doing so takes a lot of time, and you may lose potential customers. The script lets you close the room and start your confirmed buyers filling out the paperwork. Then you can go around the room and talk with them first, demonstrating to the rest that indeed people are saying yes tonight. You also know who is committed right off the bat.

"I'm going to hand out the enrollment forms. Don't worry— touching them won't charge your credit card!

By now you are in one of three different groups. The first group says, "I'm in. You had me at hello. I love this stuff and can totally see myself using it." If you're in this group, simply start filling out the shaded areas, choose a kit, and we will get you started right away.

The second group says, "I want to do this but I have a few questions." If this is you, go ahead and fill out the form, and then you and I will visit one on one, and we'll get your questions answered and pick out an enrollment kit that's right for you.

If you are in the third group, you had a great time and learned a lot, but it's not for you. That is totally fine. But maybe three or four people came to mind during the class who would enjoy coming to a future class. If you could just jot down their contact info, we will make sure we plug them into the next set of classes.

Remember, just because someone isn't filling out the paperwork does not mean they don't want to buy. They may simply have some questions or concerns, and that is okay. But get the excited ones signed up first, and then work with the others. As for those who do have questions or concerns, the next chapter is dedicated entirely to helping your customers overcome their sticking points.

ENROLL

You have explained to people how they can become involved. They understand your company's loyalty rewards program (if you have one). Now it's time to sign them up! This can be the most difficult part. It's the step in the sales cycle where presenters lose enrollments because they do not understand how people make decisions.

Many presenters tell me they simply finish explaining the kits and auto-ship program and then say, "If you have any questions, just let me know." But again, people have a difficult time making decisions on their own, especially when the information is new to them. So we need to help attendees make a decision.

We do this by taking action and going directly to the most interested person in the room. Our confidence will be the confidence they need when making a decision.

- "How did you feel about what you just experienced?"
- "Would it be okay if I shared with you how to set up a wholesale membership?"
- "Which of these options makes the most sense for your family and you?"

SOLIDIFY THE ENROLLMENT

Once you've made an enrollment, make sure you solidify it. This is where a lot of folks miss the ball: they fail to understand that people can develop buyer's remorse after making a decision.

How often have you pulled something off the shelf at the grocery store, put it in your cart, and then a few aisles later said to yourself, "You know what? I don't need this." We are good at talking ourselves out of things that often are good for us (and bad at talking ourselves out of things that are bad for us).

We need to be mindful of the situation that awaits enrollees when they get home. They may have a husband who is not happy that his wife went to our presenation in the first place. Maybe he had to put the kids to bed solo, and now he has to endure his wife's show-and-tell the minute she comes home—and usually, none of it is for him!

Here is a typical post-presentation conversation between spouses:

"Hi, honey! I'm back from the presentation."

"Uh . . . you didn't buy anything did you?"

"Well, um . . . kind of."

"What did you get this time?"

"Just some essential oils."

"Oils? We don't need oils. You don't believe in all that snake oil stuff, do you? Why did you get oils?"

"Well, I'm, uh, not sure . . . except, well, they are natural—and certified."

You know the drill. We need to empower people with information to build their confidence so their spouse does not derail the enrollment. Because the bottom line is, enrollees are trying to help their families.

A way to build confidence and solidify the enrollment is to ask the person, "Why did you end up enrolling tonight?" As she responds, have her write down her answers on her presentation handout while you take notes as well. That way, when she goes home, she can read exactly why she enrolled to her spouse. And better yet, you now have her reasons to use as a third-party testimonial—as well as backup in case she gets cold feet after entering the husband zone!

The follow-up appointment or membership overview meeting also validates the decision to buy. Set an appointment at the presentation or the following day to do a membership overview with your new customer.

WHY PEOPLE EXPERIENCE BUYER'S REMORSE

Here are some common reasons why people have second thoughts about their purchase or enrollment:

- We didn't close in the decision zone.

- Our presentation was *toooo* long.

- We didn't build a sharing environment (too much pressure).

- We forgot to say, "I just have to ask, Betty: Why did you decide to do this?"

- We didn't write down their reasons for enrolling on their enrollment form and take a picture of it so they could repeat those reasons back to their spouses.

- We didn't do a membership overview after the enrollment.

REFERRALS

How many referrals do you get after the presenation? How about the follow-up meeting after someone enrolls? When is the best time to ask? Why don't more people ask for them?

You got to the end of the presentation, you provided value, and yet some folks discovered it was not for them and left without enrolling. No problem, right?

Wrong. When people walk out of a presentation or one-on-one, anywhere from 25 to 600 other people leave with them. I once read that the average person knows 600 people and has between 10 and 25 people they trust in their network. So let's just arbitrarily choose the number 15 and multiply it by the number of people who left your last presentation without enrolling. *That is the number of potential customers you could have!* Suppose that five people leave. There are potentially 75 people who trust those five and who are great candidates for your next presentation!

What about those who do enroll? The number goes up due to the credibility of the referral. So if you have 10 people at a presentation who enroll, then there are potentially 150 other people who could be introduced to you by enrollees whom they know and trust.

Referrals are vital in your business. It has been said that God invented cold calling for people who do not ask for referrals! People buy when someone they trust reduces or eliminates the risk of purchasing in the buyer's mind. That is why third-party testimonials and stories are key. It is powerful to hear a story of someone who has had a great product experience.

So why do people avoid asking for referrals? It starts with their belief system. The word *referrals* carries a negative connotation. Many people may picture an insurance salesman hammering at them for the names of all their friends, whom the salesman wants to high-pressure into buying a policy. To avoid that negative association, while we will use the word *referral* in our discussion, you should not use it when you are talking with a customer or prospect.

WHY PEOPLE DON'T ASK FOR REFERRALS

Any or all of several factors can play into people's reluctance to ask for referrals.

They may not believe that a customer who just enrolled will share the names of their friends until *after* they have had a chance to experience the product for themselves.

They may fear that they'll mess up the sale. As one mom said, "I just had them sit through an hour-and-a-half presentation and agree to purchase a kit. I don't want to come across as pushy now and ask them for all of their friends' names."

They're afraid of touching a nerve with a customer who had a bad experience referring someone else to a friend. Let's say the vacuum cleaner salesman stopped by your customer's house two months ago, and the customer referred them to her sister, and the sister subsequently chewed out your customer for making the referral. She might have cold feet about giving another referral—and you might feel reluctant to risk asking for one.

The customer may not view sharing a referral as helping her friends. She needs to become convinced that she is doing them a good turn by helping them gain access to something that helped her. The referral-asking game can be filled with pressure if your customers focus on themselves rather than on helping their friends get the same great benefit (education at the presentation) that they have just experienced.

Finally, some people just can't think of anyone. Or if they do pass on the name of someone they know, they request that you not use their own name. That is not a referral.

Those are the obstacles; now how do we move beyond them and get referrals? It starts with getting into the right mindset. We have to believe that our customers will like us, that they will trust us, and that we can deliver an equally high level of service to their referrals. And we have to believe in our mission. It's our duty to help people help their friends acquire our solutions so we can change their lives.

Have you ever done a great presentation and had plenty of enrollments, but the next day you had to start all over because you exhausted all of your names? Referrals are an easy way to open up the conversation, take the pressure off yourself, and begin to help people help their friends.

Some of your best customers will come from people who didn't enroll or even come to a presentation—but they did refer their friends. For that matter, I've had people refer their friends and in the process talk themselves into either coming to a presentation or enrolling!

SIMPLE BRIDGE STATEMENT FOR REQUESTING A REFERRAL

Use the following script as a model for requesting referrals from your customers.

> Betty, I really appreciate working with you tonight, and I know you will love your enrollment kit.
>
> Many of the people who come to our classes get about 10 minutes in and think of several friends or family members who would also have loved to be here tonight. As a professional courtesy to people who come to my classes, we set up a class for their friends who would have wanted to come had they known how cool this was tonight.
>
> So, Betty, who came to mind during the class—friends, family, or whomever—who are just like you and whom we should be talking to? You know—they want [benefit Betty just received by signing up], just like you do.

You may need to jog their memory. People often cannot remember other people on the spot, so you'll need to jog their minds. Following is another brief script to guide you.

> As I said in the beginning of the class, people come to these classes for one of three reasons. (State those reasons; you should come up with them in advance.) Who comes to mind that we can help as well?

You can also offer suggestions: What about fellow church members? Women in their moms' group? Their massage therapist, their chiropractor, people on their softball team, and so forth?

FOLLOW UP

Some people will enroll. Some people will not enroll. What do we do with these two groups after the presentation?

You may have heard the saying "The fortune is in the follow-up." Do you have a good follow-up plan?

The following striking statistics dramatize the importance of follow-up:

- 48 percent of salespeople never follow up with a prospect.
- 25 percent of salespeople make a second contact and stop.
- 12 percent of salespeople only make three contacts and stop.
- Only 10 percent of salespeople make more than three contacts. But . . .
  - 2 percent of sales are made on the first contact.
  - 3 percent of sales are made on the second contact.
  - 5 percent of sales are made on the third contact.
  - 10 percent of sales are made on the fourth contact.
  - 80 percent of sales are made on the fifth to twelfth contact.

If this plays out as indicated, then we are all leaving a ton of enrollments on the table! According to these statistics, most people do not follow up. That is human nature. STARfish prioritize follow-up in order to increase their chances of securing an enrollment or an appointment. I would argue that the above stats reflect people who have not learned the skills and mindset you are learning by reading this book—and the lower the level of skill, the more essential follow-up becomes.

TOP REASONS FOR FOLLOW-UP

Here are nine reasons why follow-up is so important. Do any of them look familiar?

1. People had to leave early.
2. People left before they met one on one with you.
3. Needed to talk with spouse.
4. Needed to think about it.
5. "It's a bad time. Call me next month."
6. They ordered retail.
7. They wanted to think about what to order.
8. The person wanted to check with a trusted authority (e.g., their doctor, etc.).
9. They enrolled! (And you want them to stay enrolled.)

You will want to create two follow-up checklists: one for when people enroll and the other for when they do not.

Checklist for when people enroll

☐ Send a handwritten thank-you note.
☐ Make a "Welcome!" phone call.
☐ Send a "Welcome!" email with product education links.
☐ Do a membership overview.
☐ Determine if they want to be a product user or business builder.
☐ Invite them to attend a second presentation.
☐ Do an opportunity overview.

☐ Conduct a new distributor business training

☐ Make a names list and schedule first four events.

Checklist for when people do not enroll

☐ Know the *real* reason why before they leave presentation.

☐ Know their time frame for making a decision.

☐ Set a follow-up appointment at the presentation and ensure that it goes in their calendar.

☐ Write a handwritten thank-you note.

☐ Follow up with education and inspiration.

☐ Expect them to eventually become customers, and believe in them!

CHAPTER 9

PRINCIPLE 6: RESOLVE CUSTOMER CHALLENGES

Successful people focus on all of the reasons people should buy while unsuccessful people focus on all of the reasons people won't buy.

—Neal Anderson

STARfish know how to handle customer challenges. It is critical that we address potential challenges before they arise. Remember, the first one to the objection wins!

People avoid making a decision because they fear making the wrong decision. They will use any excuse they can find to protect them from the pain of going home from a presentation and being bombarded by a husband: "We don't need essential oils—we have health insurance." Or, "You didn't get suckered into buying any of that snake oil, did you?"

THE FOUR AREAS OF OBJECTION

It's helpful to know that people's objections group into just four categories. Once you recognize them, you can know how to address them. They are

1. Status quo: the customer is happy with their current product.
2. Price: the product costs too much money.
3. Spouse: a husband or wife opposes the purchase.
4. Procrastination: the customer wants to think about it.

By factoring these objections into how we structure our presentation, we can deal with them proactively. For instance, we can inform our attendees how many of the people using our products had previously been using another company's products (but be nice). We can reassure them that one of the main reasons people love using our products is because *everyone* can afford them.

We need to include a segment in the presentation that shows what men love about our products, and if possible, we should include products in our presentation that men use daily. Third-party stories are key in this segment.

What about objections during the Contact stage or at the end of a presentation? Let's say you get to the finale and someone says, "That is a lot of money." In the old-school way of handling objections, the salesperson would attempt to identify with the person's feelings: "I understand how you *feel*. I *felt* the same way until I found out that oils cost pennies per drop and actually save you money."

Today many people easily recognize this *feel, felt, found* technique, and it usually comes across as insincere. It's one thing to invite people to tap into their own emotions (e.g., "How do you feel about . . .?"); it's another thing to suggest you identify with how they feel. If you and I just met 45 minutes ago, how can I really understand how you feel? It's a bit presumptuous to say you do, especially if you're a man talking to a woman!

One of the quickest ways to lose credibility is to tell someone you understand their feelings when in fact you don't have a clue how they feel—because you haven't asked them or you just met them! Besides, people don't care how *you* feel. You are the salesperson, and they automatically distrust you because you benefit if they buy into your pitch.

The following is a better system for taking the pressure off and being authentic.

7 STEPS TO ADDRESSING OBJECTIONS

1. Focus on the benefit for the customer.
2. Identify the real issue.
3. Use a bridge statement.
4. Use a third-person "connecting" statement.
5. Use a third person to address the objection.
6. Point out how a current need can be addressed with the product.
7. Close.

Following are some basic scripts that illustrate how you might handle various objections. The first example is from the essential oil/ health and wellness industry. I'm sure it will be quite apparent how to customize these for your company, product, or service

HAPPY WITH THE CURRENT PRODUCT OR SERVICE

When people tell you they already use another competing product or are looking at one, or they ask, "How are you different," they are really saying, "Help me make a decision." We tend to go on about quality, sourcing, culture, and how great we are rather than focusing on the customer.

Next time, try the following script. Use it as a model, and adapt it to fit your company and the criteria people should use when deciding whether to join you. You'll find it's a lot more effective to teach people guidelines for making their decision, especially when those rules lead to enrolling with you.

Mrs. Customer, I know you are evaluating the best options for your family, and I really can appreciate that. Sally Johnson said this same thing last week, and what she really wanted was some criteria that she should be using to evaluate her best option.

What I said to her was, "You will want to make sure that the products are sourced from the best place in which to grow and harvest each plant. We have found through extensive research that this is one of the keys to potency. We could just grow them on a big farm or two here in the United States, but that would not be the best for our customers.

"Next, you will want to make sure that they have a stamp to ensure purity and integrity according to third-party testing.

"Finally, you will want a company that provides a holistic, big-picture approach to health and wellness by having products that address concerns that go beyond just those for which you would use essential oils. For example, you will want access to a great cleansing product to remove existing toxins from your body and optimize organ function. You want products that help

you reduce toxic load and ones that support nutrition, so you ultimately need less oils!

"When you have all of those things working together, then you have the best chance to achieve optimum health. Without those key elements, essential oils are simply not as effective. And our mission is to provide not only the highest quality essential oils but also to help people optimize their overall health, so they can do more of what they love to do with more energy and less stress."

And that is why everyone has been so excited about XYZ company!

Have fun using this script. Again, modify it to fit your circumstances—and remember to have a humble heart! You don't want to bash another company. The goal is to state criteria a customer can use to make their own mental comparison between their current product and yours—so that the logical conclusion is YOU!

So what concerns must you be prepared to address in order for people to wisely choose your company?

MONEY

Prospect: *That costs a lot of money.*

You: *I totally get it. A lot of people are pinching pennies these days and want to make sure they are spending money only on necessities. They hold off on buying things they don't need.*

Let me ask you this: Besides its being "a lot of money," is there any other reason that keeps you from enrolling?

Prospect: *No, it's just the money.*

You: Oh, good. Jenny was at a class last week and felt pretty much the same way. She said that she and her husband are cutting a lot out of the budget and trying to save money these days. One of the reasons she ended up enrolling is because she wanted to make sure she had something around the house that would save them money in the long run. *(Insert how your product can save them money, time, and so on.)*

She said she wasn't sure she had the money, but one thing was for sure: she wanted to be prepared so she didn't have to spend more money down the road. How do you think she feels now, having these products in her house?

Prospect: Better, I guess. Ready to handle upcoming challenges.

You: Exactly! That's the main reason everyone has been so excited about *[your company].* So let's go ahead and get you started. (Go right into signing them up)

SPOUSE

I can totally relate. Besides wanting to talk to your spouse, is there any other reason keeping you from enrolling?

Most of the moms are the ones who end up making the decision to get most things around the house. When they go to Target and an hour later walk out with $100 worth of stuff they didn't plan on buying, very rarely do they call their spouse from the frying pan section to see if that's what they should get.

Besides, Dad also makes his own buying decisions. One wife told me, "If he blows a tire on the way home from work or needs a new lawnmower, we don't have a family meeting to see if he is going to get a new tire or lawnmower. He simply goes and gets one. It's his department, and I trust *his decision that he will get the best tire or lawnmower. And he trusts that on my part, I will also make the best decision when evaluating things to take care of the family."*

Is that pretty much how it works in your house too? Great, so let's go ahead and get this enrollment kit shipped out so you can start using it right away. Do you get your mail at your house or the post office?"

PROCRASTINATION

I can appreciate where you are coming from. Besides wanting to think about it, is there any other reason keeping you from enrolling tonight?

Most people want to think about what they are doing to make sure they are making the best decision. We all want to make sure we are getting what we need and will use.

Based on your goals list (which the prospect wrote down during the presentation), which of your health or financial goals did you want to work on first? Why did you pick those two? If there were a kit that would help with those, would that be good to have around the house? Why?

Based on what you've told me, it sounds like [name the appropriate offering] is going to be a perfect fit for you. Go ahead and fill in your information and check this box for the kit, and we will get it sent out tomorrow.

NETWORK MARKETING/MLM CHALLENGE

I have so enjoyed this conversation and feedback! And I agree with a lot of what you've had to say. Mind if I share a few of my own perspectives?

Network marketing companies today are very different from those of our parents' generation. The legitimate ones are not a get-rich-quick scheme but are based on service and consumption. What I mean is, they give you the option to buy something unique from another person, often another mom like yourself, rather than from a big-box store. You get an equal, and often superior, product from the mom. Kind of like the whole concept of buying local.

The struggle comes into play when salespeople act like fire hoses, spewing information and their product all over their Facebook page or every conversation you have with them. That's why I personally swore I would never be a part of network marketing.

But I found a product I love and use every day, and that gives me the opportunity to truly help other people by sharing it with them.

In just two years, I have been able to completely replace my husband's corporate six-figure income and enabled him to come work with me full time.

Now we do this as a family, helping to empower and transform other people's health and finances. It has allowed me to stay at home with our kids.

Before I had kids, I was an executive recruiter. We would never have hired an accountant who didn't have accounting experience or a lawyer without a law degree. If you don't have some business or sales background and want to supplement your income with network marketing or any sales job, then you should learn some basic sales skills. And you can learn them—but you have to put forth the effort.

Whether you realize it or not, we are all in network marketing to some degree. It's just that very few people get paid for it. How many times have you asked your waitress what her favorite dish is? Or asked someone for a great book suggestion? How about a good movie? You were going to eat a meal, read a book, and see a movie regardless of what those people said, but their recommendation influenced your choice. However, none of them got compensated for sharing with you what they enjoyed. That's just not how restaurants, bookstores, and movie theaters are set up.

For all the mommies who are part of direct selling/network marketing and don't want to be that friend whom people run from: have a heart of service. When your heart is on service, you cannot be nervous. I would rather mention what I do, educate people on alternatives, and have people say no than never say anything at all. I consider myself the messenger, and what others do with that information is up to them.

This last, heartfelt scenario comes to you courtesy of Erin Anderson, my wife.

ASSIGNMENT

- Write out answers to the most common objections for your product.
- Find third-party testimonials of people who overcame these objections.
- With another person, practice responding with your answers and testimonials, and commit them to memory.

BEING THE STARfish™

I t was a year later, and once again Sellfy was sitting across from Sherri in her home office. But what a difference that year had made! A difference in Sellfy's volume, beyond a doubt, but most of all, a difference in Sellfy.

Sherri smiled at him. "I wonder if you have any idea just how much you've changed, Sellfy. That guy who walked in here a year back was broken and yet prideful. The man I'm looking at now is confident yet humble. And, I might add, servant-hearted—and successful."

It was true. Following all of the principles Sherri had guided him through, Sellfy had transformed his business and had a wonderful time in the process. People were now drawn to Sellfy. He loved how he was changing lives by helping people not only enjoy the benefits of his products but also share them with other people. He loved making a real difference. Sellfy was no longer a SELLfish. He had become Sellfy the STARfish!

"I couldn't have done it without you, Sherri," he gratefully admitted. "I owe you so much."

"You owe me nothing except to pass on the blessing," Sherri replied. "You're ready. You became coachable. You worked hard. And you understand that there are no shortcuts, just a system that works if you follow it."

"It sure does," Sellfy said. "And I'm amazed how much fun it's been. I would love to help others learn how to do what I do. I can't imagine anything more rewarding than watching them grow and reach for their dreams. So how do I go about it?"

"It's time to get you into the leadership program. Time to help you inspire a team and change their lives just like yours has been changed. Meet me back here a year from now and we will get to work."

Sherri's smile broadened. "Until then, Mr. STARfish, go change the world one person at a time. And remember, the answer lies behind the next door. You just have to knock."

STARFISH™ VERSUS SELLFISH

STARFISH

- Extremely coachable
- Works a schedule
- Extremely positive
- Leads with product
- Focuses on sowing
- Focuses on activity
- Asks questions to create a need
- Creates a sharing environment
- Has a vision for their life
- Finds a way
- Controls the controllables
- Leaves everyone in a great mood
- Uses third-person stories
- Invests back into their business
- Knows and applies the sales cycle
- Always finds out, "How did you hear about our company?"

SELLFISH

- Knows it all
- Wings it
- Glass is half empty
- Leads with opportunity
- Focuses on selling
- Focuses on sales
- Knows it all
- Creates pressure
- Has no long-term vision
- Finds an excuse
- Focuses on things they can't control
- Is frustrated with rejection
- Fails to use third-person stories
- Complains about investing in their business
- Reinvents the wheel
- Cross-recruits—enrolls other people's people

ACKNOWLEDGEMENTS

I felt an intense sense of accomplishment when I finished my last edit. There had been many sleepless nights, missed meals, nights I did not read with my kids or have dinner with my wife. Now the book is finished, it's time to say a few thank-yous. I have ample reasons to feel grateful toward a number of people in my life.

Before I thank those people specifically, though, I want to say thanks to all of the people behind the tens of thousands of doors on which I have knocked. Your yeses paid my bills. Your noes built my character and gave me the experience with which I can help others. Without the opportunities you gave me to face my fears during those 50,000 sales calls, I would not be who I am today. You were my laboratory of life. You allowed me to gain a unique perspective by meeting with you in your living rooms, on your front porches, under carports, and in your offices. Thank you.

Thank you to my friends at Southwestern Advantage, especially the late Creig Soeder, who gave me the opportunity, back in my days as a college and law student, to knock on all of those doors.

Thank you to our company and all of our friends in the business and those whom we have met in other companies along the way. We truly have a great profession! Keep moving it forward and bringing others with you. We are truly better when we bloom where we are planted.

Thank you to the members of the STARfish Community. You are some of my biggest cheerleaders. Your support has meant the world to me as we have built this movement.

Thank you so much Tom, Cathleen, Chris, Beth, and Megan Connolly. You are my second family, and I so much appreciate your generosity and all you have done for me. Working on this book while sitting in your Adirondack camp in Lake Pleasant, New York, was one of the highlights of this journey.

Thank you to Suzi Overstreet, Bob Hartig, and Frank Gutbrod for your great work illustrating, editing, and laying out the book. I could not have done this without you. Looking forward to the next one! A special thank you to Suzi and her husband Joel for leading the STARfish marketing and Events team. You are a special couple.

To Mom and Dad, who were always there when I didn't know where I was! You are two STARfish who will go down in the STARfish Hall of Fame.

Thank you to my family. To my three young men, CJ, Spencer, and Thomas: You have what it takes. I love you.

Erin, you are the greatest STARfish I know and an even better friend and wife. Thank you for your patience and willingness not only to put up with me, but for all you do to make our family tick.

Finally, thank you Jesus for saving me and giving me a second chance in life, and then enabling me to help others.

BOOKS TO READ

- The Bible
- *The Ragamuffin Gospel*—Brennen Manning
- *Mere Christianity*—C.S. Lewis
- *Golf's Sacred Journey*—David L. Cook
- *It's Your Call*—Gary Barkalow
- *The Heart of a Warrior*—Michael Thompson
- *Wild at Heart*—John Eldridge
- *Captivating*—Stasi Eldridge
- *Love and Respect*—Dr. Emerson Eggerichs
- *The Greatest Salesman in the World*—Og Mandino
- *7 Habits of Highly Effective People*—Stephen Covey
- *How to Win Friends and Influence People*—Dale Carnegie
- *The Magic of Thinking Big*—David Schwartz
- *4 Arguments for the Elimination of Television*—Jerry Mander
- *The Common Denominator of Success*—Albert Gray
- *The Rich Dad's Cashflow Quadrant*—Robert Kiyosaki
- *Purposed Linked Organization*—Alaina Love and Marc Cugnon
- *Emotional Intelligence*—Daniel Goleman
- *The Millionaire Mind*—Stanley Danko
- *Start with Why*—Simon Sinek
- *Leaders Eat Last*—Simon Sinek

- *The Invisible Touch*—Harry Beckwith
- *Launching a Leadership Revolution*—Orrin Woodward and Chris Brady
- *The Leadership Train*—Orrin Woodward
- *Rascal*—Chris Brady
- *Slight Edge*—Jeff Olson
- *Go Pro*—Eric Worre
- *The Four Year Career*—Richard Brooke
- *Rock Your Network Marketing Business*—Sarah Robbins
- *Making the First Circle Work*—Randy Gage
- *The Compound Effect*—Darren Hardy
- *Last Child in the Woods: Saving Our Children from Nature Deficit Disorder*—Richard Louv
- *The Wright Brothers*—David McCullough